The
HERMITAGE

The History
of the Buildings
and
Collections

ALFA-COLOUR ART PUBLISHERS
ST PETERSBURG
2000

August 2001

Foreword by MIKHAIL PIOTROVSKY

Introductory articles by LIUDMILA TORSHINA
Notes on the plates by SOPHIA KUDRIAVTSEVA

Translation from the Russian by PAUL WILLIAMS
(foreword and introductory articles)
and VALERY FATEYEV (notes on the plates)

Design by VASILY BERTELS

Photographs by DARYA BOBROVA, LEONID BOGDANOV,
PAVEL DEMIDOV, ALEXANDER KASHNITSKY,
LEONARD KHEIFETS, YURY MOLODKOVETS,
VICTOR SAVIK, YEVGENY SHLEPKIN, YEVGENY SINIAVER,
GEORGY SKACHKOV, SVETLANA SUETOVA,
VLADIMIR TEREBENIN AND OLEG TRUBSKY

Colour correction by VLADIMIR AND PETER KRAKOVSKY

Managing editor NINA GRISHINA

Colour-separated films by AMOS, St Petersburg
PRINTED AND BOUND IN FINLAND

ISBN 5-900959-38-4

The
HERMITAGE

The History
of the Buildings
and
Collections

The Hermitage

Hermitage, the world-renowned art museum on the banks of the River Neva, is the pride of Russia and its northern capital, St Petersburg. It contains incalculable treasures of world culture. In the Hermitage collections there are some three million separate items. They are works of art and culture of the peoples of East and West spanning an immense period of time from deep antiquity to the twentieth century. All forms of artistic creativity, a multitude of different facets of world culture, are represented in the museum's stocks. Archaeological items inform us about the oldest cultures of the Ancient World, the East and Russia. Extremely rich collections of paintings, graphic art and sculpture give an outstanding picture of the history of fine art from the rock drawings of primitive peoples to the painted vases and sculpture of the Ancient Greeks and Romans, from early Christian art – the Fayum portraits and Byzantine icons – to the great masters of the Italian Renaissance, from the Classical schools of the seventeenth century – the "Golden Age" of Western European art – to the French Impressionists and the leading figures of the twentieth century, from the painting of China and Tibet to the miniatures of India and Iran. The wealth of the Hermitage's collections of applied art is inexhaustible – Ancient pottery and Chinese porcelain, the gold of the Scythians and the Ancient Greeks, Persian carpets and European tapestries, the silver of the remote Sassanid kingdom and of the eighteenth-century craftsmen of Paris and Augsburg, clothing, furniture, jewellery and much else besides. Almost a million coins and medals, from ancient times to the present day, belong to the Hermitage's numismatic department. Glistening in this vast "ocean" are the masterpieces of Leonardo da Vinci, Titian, Giorgione, Raphael, Rembrandt, Rubens, Van Dyck, Velázquez, Monet, Renoir, Cézanne, Van Gogh, Gauguin, Matisse, Picasso...

One further unique quality of the Hermitage is the buildings in which it is situated. They are outstanding monuments of Russian architecture and history. The museum's main displays occupy the main palatial ensemble in St Petersburg: the Winter Palace — residence of the Russian emperors — and the adjoining Small, Old and Large Hermitages together with the Hermitage Theatre. Only recently the Hermitage was also given the eastern part of the tremendous General Staff building on Palace Square, while one of the sections of the museum is located on the opposite bank of the Neva, in the palace of St Petersburg's first governor, the Most Illustrious Prince Menshikov. The elegant Hermitage buildings,

Panoramic
view of the Hermitage
from the Neva

where the historical appearance of the interiors has been excellently preserved, provide a noble setting for the museum's art collections.

In the mind of every visitor who comes into the Hermitage and strolls around its beautiful halls, admiring the creation of skilled human hands, the question probably arises: how did this museum appear and from where; how did it happen that in distant Russia, on the fringes of Europe, in one of the continent's youngest cities, this superb repository of artistic treasures, one of the world's greatest, was created?

Every era has made its contribution to the formation of the Hermitage. Catherine's heirs turned "her Hermitage" – the object of the Empress's personal amusements and enthusiasms – into a superbly organized museum. The construction of the New Hermitage to house the collections in the mid-nineteenth century made it possible to open the first public museum in Russia – the Imperial Hermitage. The era of the Imperial Hermitage gave way in the early twentieth century to the era of the State Hermitage. Having become the property of the nation as a result of revolution, in the complex, at times dramatic conditions of the post-revolutionary period, the Second World War, and post-war reconstruction, the Hermitage managed to increase its artistic wealth many times over and to become one of the greatest centres of culture in Russia and the world.

The process of creating the Hermitage is continuing today: the collections are being enlarged, the complex of buildings expanded, the halls restored, new displays opened. Right now a tremendous project is under way to turn the Hermitage into a twenty-first century museum – the "Great Hermitage". In the near future the Hermitage will occupy a number of historical buildings on Palace Square, to be linked to the established Hermitage buildings by an underground passageway. The museum's galleries and displays will combine with lecture halls, theatres and concerts halls, electronic information and electronic art centres, museum libraries, cafés and restaurants. This tremendous centre of museum and artistic culture, the Hermitage and Palace Square, will become in the twenty-first century the living heart of St Petersburg.

Mikhail Piotrovsky

Director of the Hermitage, Professor of Historical Sciences,
Corresponding Member of the Russian Academy of Sciences
and the Russian Academy of Arts

The
HERMITAGE

*The Age
of Catherine the Great:
The 18th Century*

RASTRELLI AND
THE WINTER PALACE

*Portrait
of Empress Elizabeth
Petrovna*
By an unknown artist
active in the late 1750s
Mosaic

◀The Main (Jordan) Staircase
of the Winter Palace
By Bartolomeo Francesco
Rastrelli, 1754–61;
restored by Vasily Stasov,
1838–39

◀◀ *Portrait
of Empress Catherine
the Great*
By Johann-Baptist Lampi
the Elder. 1793
Oil on canvas

In January 1752, on the day after seeing in the New Year, Her Majesty Empress Elizabeth, dissatisfied with the cramped conditions that she had been obliged to experience in her palace during the celebrations, gave orders for her court architect-in-chief, Count de Rastrelli, to draw up plans for the reconstruction and enlargement of her winter residence in Saint Petersburg.

The existing Winter Palace had been constructed back in the early 1730s, for Empress Anna Ioannovna, and was, strictly speaking, from the outset not a royal palace. During the early years after the foundation of Saint Petersburg in 1703, leading figures in Peter the Great's circle had built their houses on this stretch of the embankment, close to the Tsar's own modest Winter Palace on the south bank of the great River Neva. The largest and most attractive of those mansions belonged to Admiral General Fiodor Apraxin. When he died without heirs, Apraxin bequeathed his house to the imperial family. Anna Ioannovna, Peter's niece, gave orders for it to be reconstructed into a Winter Palace for her own use. The work was entrusted to the Rastrellis, father and son.

Rastrelli senior, Carlo Bartolomeo (1675–1744), was an Italian, one among the foreign artists that Peter the Great eagerly invited to his new capital. He came to Russia in 1716 from Paris where he had been unsuccessfully seeking suitable employment. It was in the French capital that his son, Bartolomeo Francesco (1700–1771) destined to become a great Russian architect, had been born. At the age of sixteen, then, after a basic artistic education in France, Rastrelli junior found himself in Russia. As his father's pupil and assistant, he participated in the drawing up of architectural plans. Although Carlo Bartolomeo made his name in his new country chiefly as an outstanding sculptor (the equestrian statue of Peter the Great that can now be seen in front of the Mikhailovsky Castle, *Empress Anna with a Negro Boy Servant*, busts of Peter himself and his closest comrade-in-arms, Alexander Menshikov), he was quite often called on to exercise his skills as an architect as well.

In this field of endeavour, however, the son far outshone the father. The skills of an architect and the fantasy of an artist combined in Bartolomeo Francesco with profound knowledge of different styles. In his work he drew on the lessons in French Classicism that he received in his youth, on the principles of the Italian Baroque (Rastrelli studied in Italy for five years, from 1725 to 1730), and on the traditions of Early Russian architecture. The majestic cathedrals of Moscow's Kremlin and monasteries and the white-stone churches of old Russian cities had impressed the young future architect on the long journey from Moscow to newly-founded Saint Petersburg. All this came together to make Rastrelli a Russian architect of European magnitude, the creator of an original style — the Russian Baroque. The distinctive features of that style manifested themselves already in the 1730s during the creation of Anna Ioannovna's palace, where Rastrelli junior directed the main work. Over many subsequent years he repaired and refurbished the palace as it became necessary, incorporated adjoining buildings into it and added new wings. Small wonder, then, that twenty years later, in the reign of Empress Elizabeth, the old Winter Palace presented in the words of one historian "a motley, dirty appearance, unworthy of the site it occupied, and the very strangeness of the palace could not have been pleasing to the Empress."

Empress Elizabeth, moreover, was not the princess of a small German state as Anna Ioannovna had remained in her mental attitude even when on the Russian throne. The daughter of Peter the Great, brought to the throne in November 1741 in a palace coup led by the guards, Elizabeth continued her father's policies aimed at strengthening Russia and her own autocratic rule. Russia's victories in wars with Sweden and Prussia, its growing European importance, the first green shoots of the Enlightenment – the founding of Moscow University, the Academy of Arts and a national theatre – all bolstered her authority. Elizabeth's court still retained something of patriarchal Muscovy. However, the customs of the pious past – journeys on pilgrimage and calling on her subjects "for tea" – alternated with ever more magnificent formal receptions and public outings, opulent celebrations, balls, masquerades and theatrical performances. The "greatness of the imperial dignity", as Elizabeth's decree put it, dictated the need to reconstruct the Winter Palace "with greater space in length, breadth and height".

On 16 June 1754 the architectural plans were approved and a body was set up to oversee the construction In the course of the work on the project Rastrelli's grand concept for an enormous edifice matured and, with the Empress's support, on 7 May 1775 the architect set about realizing it. For six years, uninterrupted summer and winter, in defiance of the sharp Russian frosts and snow, building work continued. Carts dragged slowly to Saint Petersburg one after another. Barges brought stone and sand, chalsk and bricks down the Neva. More than 4,000 men laboured on the construction site. In the spring of 1761 the shell of the building was completed and work on the decoration of the interior began. An elegant, majestic palace had appeared in the centre of Saint Petersburg – a splendid example of the Russian Baroque. Bartolomeo Francesco Rastrelli's last and most perfect creation.

*Portrait
of the Architect Bartolomeo
Francesco Rastrelli*
BY AN UNKNOWN ARTIST ACTIVE
IN THE MID-18TH CENTURY
Oil on canvas

The Winter Palace fitted superbly into the unique cityscape of the new Russian capital. The powerful race of waves on the Neva echoes the rhythm of the snow-white columns on the northern façade of the palace. Projecting elements in the eastern and western façades make the building reach out to the city: the eastern ones were later concealed by the Small Hermitage, those on the west still overlook the old building of the Admiralty. The southern façade, though, is the grandest and most opulent. On that side the palace is open to the extensive square to which it has given a name: columns are distributed along the whole of its immense length, alone, in pairs, in tight groups, enlivening the surface of the wall with an impression of unhurried, somewhat wave-like movement. The triple arch that forms the entrance to the inner courtyard with its wrought-iron gates shows the route the imperial carriages would have taken conveying the owners and the from the palace, while from the low stone balustrade encircling the roof mighty ancient gods, heroes and milirary commanders look down on Saint Petersburg in the form of statues and busts created to Rastrelli's designs.

Nowadays, only a very few rooms in the Winter Palace retain Rastrelli's Baroque decoration as an enduring, visible reminder of the size and scope of his concept. Much of the north-eastern corner of the great building is taken up by the Main Staircase. Ascending its steps, you suddenly emerge from the semi-gloom of the vaults below into an immense, glowing space. There, at a height of almost twenty metres the gods of Olympus hover in azure sky of the painted ceiling. Light pours through the windows and, reflecting in the mirrors, caresses the white walls, the gilded mouldings and the statues of gods and muses.

In the south-east corner Rastrelli placed the palace church. This place of Russian Orthodox worship, crowned in observance of tradition with a dome, was decorated effectively as yet another state room with unrestrained Baroque splendour, a physical expression of exultant joy and triumph.

Empress Elizabeth did not, however, live to move into her new palace. She died on 25 December 1761. The owner of the unfinished palace was now the new emperor, Elizabeth's nephew and designated heir, Peter III. Suspending work on the state rooms, Rastrelli urgently decorated living apartments for Peter III. The immense expanse of the square below the Emperor's windows was crowded with stores, barracks, piles of brick and stone, building timber and just plain rubbish. The head of the city police had it announced that anybody could come and take what he wanted. In a matter of hours "not a single stone or brick, nor one board" remained on the square. In April 1762 Peter III moved into the incomplete Winter Palace. In June another palace coup brought a new empress – Catherine II – to the Russian throne and a new chapter in the history of the imperial winter residence began – the story of the Hermitage.

1
**View of the Winter Palace
from Vasilyevsky Island**

The banks of the Neva afford a magnificent view of Palace Bridge
and Palace Embankment. The façades of the Hermitage complex,
which deservedly rank with the best architectural ensembles
of St Petersburg, run alongside the embankment.
The Winter Palace, the official residence
of the Russian imperial family, was put up by the architect
Bartolomeo Francesco Rastrelli in 1754–62.
Linked with the other buildings of the Hermitage museum
by covered passageways, it is the focus of the brilliant ensemble
created in the course of a century.
The façade of the palace, extending for 200 metres, and decorated
with dozens of white columns and a great number of statues,
vases and ornaments, is an illustrious example of Rastrelli's
St Petersburg Baroque style.

2
View of the Neva from the roof of the Winter Palace

According to Rastrelli's plan, the façades of the Winter Palace were crowned with a luxurious Baroque balustrade bearing numerous decorative statues and vases carved in stone. Sculptors, Rastrelli's assistants, began to work on them in 1755, and six years later the statues were mounted on the roof of the palace. A disastrous fire completely destroyed the interiors of the palaces in 1837. Some details of the decoration, such as a number of the statues on the Admiralty side of the building, were also badly damaged. Vasily Stasov, who supervised the restoration work, hired experienced craftsmen and the original appearance of the balustrade of the Winter Palace was soon restored.

3
View of the Peter and Paul Fortress from the roof of the Winter Palace

St Petersburg was founded by Peter the Great not only as the new capital of Russia but also as a major Russian port having an outlet to the sea. It was not a mere chance that the Peter and Paul Fortress became the first centre of the burgeoning capital, a core around which the city began to shape. Rastrelli selected for the royal residence that part of Admiralty Island on the opposite bank of the Neva where some palaces of the nobility have already been built. The statues of Neptune, the chief marine deity of the Romans, and his suite adorning the roof of the Winter Palace, had, in addition to their decorative function, an important ideological significance — it emphasized the proximity of the official royal residence to the sea.

4
**View of the dome of the Large Church
over the Winter Palace**

The gilded dome of the Large Church glistening over the Winter Palace
is a highlight dominating the south-eastern part of its façade
overlooking Palace Square.
After the fire of 1837 the architect Vasily Stasov, who headed the
reconstruction of the Winter Palace, recreated the original appearance
of the church which had been altered after Rastrelli's death.
Thus, long before the fire the dome had been closed up inside
and the ceiling was made flat. Rastrelli's drawings were used to reconstruct
the drum, the essential symbolic element of the Orthodox church.

5
Statues
on the balustrade
of the Winter Palace

Originally the statues set on
the balustrade of the Winter
Palace had been made of soft
and porous Pudost limestone.
Over the time, affected by the
austere and changing climate
of the capital, the stone began
to crumble, flake and darken
and therefore in 1892–94
the statues were replaced
by copper casts, hollow inside.
Some details were hand-
embossed, in some other cases
the technique of galvanoplasty
was used. To ensure the
durability of the statues, they
were strengthened with steel
frames inside.

6
Decorative sculptures
on the roof
of the Winter Palace,
with a view
of St Isaac's Cathedral

Starting in 1976, a complete
restoration of the statuary
decorating the roof of the
Winter Palace is under way
in the Hermitage. Every year,
in spring, a team of metal-
workers, after covering the
copper figures with protective
plywood structures, undertake
a careful study checking the
state of their surfaces and
inner steel frames, replacing
or strengthening their affected
parts, correcting depressions
and cleaning their surfaces
from corrosion and dirt.
As a result a crust of natural
greenish-grey patina forms on
the copper surface, which not
only protects the metal from
destruction but lends it a noble
look harmonizing well with
the colour of the walls.

10 ▶

**The State Staircase
of the Winter Palace
BY BARTOLOMEO FRANCESCO
RASTRELLI (1700–1771)**

The State Staircase of the Winter Palace was designed by Rastrelli. After the fire of 1837 Vasily Stasov largely preserved its magnificent Baroque interior intact. The austere, shaded first flight of the staircase contrasts with its basic space poured with light, reflected and extended in mirrors and the illusory ceiling painting. In the eighteenth century the walls of the staircase were embellished with decorative sculpture and gilded moulding; the balusters of the handrails were also gilded. The ceiling vaults at the landing of the first floor rested on double columns of pink artificial marble. When restoring the interior after the fire, Vasily Stasov removed the lower tier of windows to enhance lighting contrasts, installed monolithic columns of grey Serdobolye granite instead of light pink columns and replaced carved

7

**The State Staircase
of the Winter Palace
BY BARTOLOMEO FRANCESCO
RASTRELLI (1700–1771)
View from the Rastrelli Gallery**

8, 9 ▶

**Statue: *Domination*
Early 18th century
BY ALVISE TAGLIAPIETRA
(1670–1747) (?)**
Marble

The statue was evidently purchased by Prince Alexander Menshikov in Venice in 1717–18 and at first stood in the garden of the Menshikov Palace. Later it was moved to the Summer Gardens and after the fire of 1837 placed in the niche of the State Staircase, since all the sculpture which had decorated the staircase perished in fire. Judging by the attributes – a crown, scales and a sword – the sculpture is an allegory of Justice rather than Domination.

and gilded balusters by a heavy marble balustrade. Instead of the burnt ceiling painting Stasov found in the storerooms of the Winter Palace a painting showing Greek gods on Olympus, a work of the eighteenth-century Italian painter Gasparo Dizziani. But since the new ceiling painting turned out to be shorter than the earlier one, the remaining space was painted "according to the former style".

13 ▶
**The Great Church of the Winter Palace
Interior**
BY BARTOLOMEO FRANCESCO RASTRELLI
(1700–1771)
(Room 271)

The Great Church, which received a status
of Cathedral in 1807, was consecrated
in 1762 to the Resurrection of Christ.
In 1763, when an image of the Saviour
was transferred to the church,
it was consecrated again, this time
as the Church of the Image of the Vernicle.
The monumental frescoes by the Italian
artist Francesco Fontebasso, the figures
of the Evangelists on the pendentives
and the composition *The Resurrection
of Christ* which had decorated the flat
ceiling of the parvis, perished in fire
and were painted anew by the Russian
artists Fiodor Bruni and Piotr Basin.
A considerable part of the church decor
was executed in papier-mâché.
This material, used instead of labour-
consuming carved wood, proved very
suitable for accelerating the restoration
of the palace after the fire.
In the 1940s the most important element
of the church decoration – the magnificent
carved iconostasis by the master
craftsman P. Cretan – was dismantled.

◀ 12
**The Great Church of the Winter Palace
Contemporary interior**

11 ▶
**The Great Church of the Winter Palace
The dome**
BY BARTOLOMEO FRANCESCO RASTRELLI
(1700–1771)

The inside of the copper gilded dome including
the lantern crowning it, was adorned, according
to Rastrelli's desire, "with ornaments,
putti, cherubs and vessels – all painted in grey
monochrome or *grisaille* and the flowers
in natural colours."

THE FOUNDATION
OF THE HERMITAGE

The spring of 1763 found the court and all the St Petersburg nobility in the old Russian capital, Moscow, where, following tradition, they were preparing for the coronation of the new empress, Catherine II. The magnificent splendour that attended that sacred event is still evident today in the luxurious coronation carriage in which Catherine entered the Kremlin. Yet in all the fuss attending the celebrations, the Empress found time to give some important instructions regarding her residence in Saint Petersburg. Among other things, she ordered the construction of a "hermitage" adjoining the Winter Palace

The fashion for "hermitages" – cosy pavilions set in the depths of a park or garden and intended for the amusement of a small, select company – had reached Russia from Europe back in the reign of Peter the Great. Catherine had fond memories of Empress Elizabeth's Hermitage at Peterhof from her young days spent there. When she became empress, Catherine decided to copy the idea at the Winter Palace. It proved quite difficult as the palace had no garden, being surrounded by the river, parade ground and neighbouring buildings. Then the new architect-in-chief Yury Velten (1730–1801) constructed a hanging garden tight up against the eastern façade of the palace, using a draft project by the French architect Jean-Baptiste Vallin de la Mothe (1729–1800) who had recently entered Russian service. At one end Velten constructed a pavilion linked to the Winter Palace by a passage – the present-day Southern Pavilion of the Small Hermitage. In Catherine's time it was known as "the Nearby House", or sometimes "the favourites' block" on account of its occupants. On the other side of the Hanging Garden in 1767–69 Velten, again working to Vallin de la Mothe's plan, constructed the northern pavilion overlooking the Neva. It was this structure that contained Catherine's "hermitage".

Nowadays, when we enter the Northern Pavilion of the Small Hermitage, we find ourselves in the elegant, spacious Pavilion Hall. This interior was created later, in the mid-nineteenth century, in place of the suite of rooms from Catherine's time. Then in the centre of the pavilion was a stateroom with windows facing the Neva. Adjoining it to the south was the Orangery that gave access to the Hanging Garden. Catherine was fond of unwinding here in quiet solitude, listening to the bubbling fountain with goldfish in its jasper basin and admiring the rare plants and brightly-coloured "American" birds. In the corners of the pavilion were small rooms, one of which was Catherine's "hermitage" or "refuge of seclusion". The two tables, each for six persons, could be laid in the kitchens on the floor below and raised into place by a special mechanism, thus sparing the party the presence of servants. Dinners here were followed by the amusing "hermitage gatherings".

Invitations to these private soirées with "theatrical performances, games and dances" were only issued to those whose company and conversation Catherine enjoyed. They were supposed to forget about affairs of state and behave in a relaxed, friendly manner. The Empress even drew up a humorous code of conduct for her guests. It was inscribed on a board by the entrance. Transgressors were to be punished by, for example, having to drink a glass of cold water or, far worse, having to learn by heart several lines from a tragedy written by the Russian poet Trediakovsky in very difficult language.

Catherine surrounded herself in the Hermitage with splendid works of art and rare, precious articles… Nowadays, the Pavilion Hall houses the Peacock Clock that Catherine inherited from Prince Grigory Potemkin, one of her favourites and the commander of the Russian army. He bequeathed the Empress his collection of art, including *Cupid Untying the Girdle of Venus* by the famous English painter Sir Joshua Reynolds. Paintings were the most valuable part of Catherine II's art collections, the museum that, like the building, came to be known as the Hermitage.

The museum had its origins in 1764 and the acquisition of a sizeable group of paintings from the Berlin merchant Gotzkowsky. Deeply in debt to the Russian treasury, he offered in settlement the collection that he had assembled for Frederick William of Prussia, but the King was unable to pay for. There were 225 works by seventeenth-century Dutch and Flemish artists, including one of the Hermitage's first masterpieces – Frans Hals's *Portrait of a Young Man with a Glove*.

The collecting of works of art had begun in Russia back in the reign of Peter the Great. The Tsar collected rarities, "curious objects" and paintings, primarily Dutch works, including Russia's first acquaintance with the great Rembrandt: his *Parting of David and Jonathan,* now in the Hermitage. Under Peter and his daughter Elizabeth, however, paintings served above all as decoration for the palaces. Catherine's idea was incomparably greater in scale and significance: after acquiring Gotzkowsky's collection, the Empress set herself the goal of creating a picture gallery, a palace museum like those that already existed at many European courts. Educated in the spirit of the latest thinking of the age (her favourite reading from early on was the works of the French Enlightenment), Catherine strove to build a reputation as an enlightened monarch. She encouraged science and art, took part in Russian literary life and corresponded with men of letters. The museum she envisaged was supposed to add lustre to her reign and raise Russia's cultural prestige.

Gotzkowsky's collection was followed by many other acquisitions. Catherine strove to create in a short time a gallery of European standard and did not count the cost. Unafraid to confess her own ignorance about paintings, Catherine skilfully selected her advisors and agents. They included several celebrated figures of the Enlightenment endowed with taste, knowledge and intuition: the philosopher and art critic Denis Diderot, the writer Melchior Grimm and the sculptor Etienne Maurice Falconet.

A particularly significant role in the creation of the Hermitage picture gallery was played by Prince Dmitry Golitsyn (1734–1803). One of the most enlightened Russians of Catherine's time, a refined connoisseur of art, Golitsyn was a diplomat, ambassador first in Paris, then, from 1768, in The Hague. He carefully followed events on the European art markets, kept in close touch and on friendly terms with scholars and collectors, and missed no opportunity to make a good purchase. It is to Golitsyn that the Hermitage is indebted for one of its most celebrated exhibits – Rembrandt's *Return of the Prodigal Son*. He first noticed the painting in 1764 at the sale of the Archbishop of Cologne's collection in Paris, where the work, now acknowledged as one of the artist's finest, did not attract the buyers' attention. In 1767, after discovering that the painting was in the hands of the Parisian collector d'Amezune, Golitsyn bought it for the Hermitage. After moving to The Hague, the Prince was very active on the art markets of the Low Countries. In 1768 he bought the collection of Count Cobenzl, a minister of the Austrian court – only forty-six paintings, but of superb quality, including as well as Flemish and Dutch works, some by old German masters that were rarely seen at the time. As well as the paintings, 4,000 drawings were acquired in the Cobenzl purchase, laying the foundations of the Hermitage's collection in that sphere of art.

The stocks of drawings and paintings were substantially enlarged in 1769 with the purchase in Dresden from the heirs of the Saxon minister Count Brühl of more than 1000 drawings and some 600 paintings, mainly by Flemish and Dutch masters. Many of them became the pride of the Hermitage, including Rembrandt's *Portrait of an Old Man in Red*; *Perseus and Andromeda* and *Landscape with a Rainbow* by Peter Paul Rubens, the creator of the seventeenth-century Flemish school. Some of the German and French works in the Brühl collection were also of excellent quality.

When living in The Hague, Prince Golitsyn remained in contact with Paris, keeping abreast of artistic life there. In 1770 Golitsyn and Diderot between them persuaded François Tronchin, a Genevan collector with close ties to Parisian colleagues, to sell the one hundred paintings he owned. Later Tronchin himself became the initiator of the most important of all the Hermitage's acquisitions to be in Catherine's reign – the famous Crozat collection.

The collection of Pierre Crozat (1665–1740) was one of the best in Paris in the first half of the seventeenth century, only the royal collections were superior to it. The catalogues listed more than

Portrait of the Architect Yury Velten
BY LUDWIG CHRISTINECK. 1770s
Oil on canvas

**The Pavilion Hall
in the Small Hermitage.
The place occupied by
the Orangery during the reign
of Catherine the Great**

400 paintings and almost 19,000 drawings. In 1772 they were acquired from his heirs for Catherine's picture gallery. (In 1778 the highly celebrated cameos from the "Cabinet de Crozat" also came into the Hermitage.)

The acquisition of the Crozat collection enriched the Hermitage with a host of first-rate works, standing out like precious gems among which were masterpieces by great artists: Rubens's *Bacchus* and *Portrait of a Maid of Honour*, as well as his sketches for the famous *Life of Marie de' Medici* series now in the Louvre in Paris; five Van Dycks, including a self-portrait; and seven Rembrandts, including the celebrated *Danaë* and *The Holy Family*.

The Hermitage's Italian stocks acquired a particular lustre. Many of the famous masterpieces of the Italian Renaissance in the museum came from the Crozat collection – *Judith*, which Crozat himself and his contemporaries considered to be by Raphael, but has since been proved to be a rare work by the Venetian painter Giorgione; Titian's *Danaë*, which in Crozat's Cabinet had hung next to Rembrandt's; canvases by Titian's celebrated pupils Veronese (*The Lamentation of Christ*) and Tintoretto (*The Nativity of John the Baptist*); and much else besides.

The Russian monarch's conspicuous acquisitions excited attention and interest. They were written about in the press, discussed in salons. In 1778 the heir of prime-minister Sir Robert Walpole approached the Russian ambassador in London with an offer to sell Catherine the collection he had inherited. Walpole's collection, kept in the family's stately home, Houghton Hall, was one of the finest in England. Its 198 paintings superbly filled out the picture gallery with works by seventeenth-century Italian artists, of which it was short, more canvases by Rembrandt and Rubens and others by the Frenchmen Nicolas Poussin and Claude Lorrain. The work of the Flemish master of the still life Frans Snyders was now represented in the Hermitage by his celebrated *Shops*, a series painted for the Bishop of Bruges. The Van Dyck collection acquired formal portraits of the English aristocracy that Walpole in his time had bought from the last Lord Wharton. The Walpole collection also brought the Hermitage a number of Spanish paintings. That important national school was little known at that time in the rest of Europe and such works were a rarity. There were relatively few Spanish paintings in Catherine's collection, but they were works of the greatest figures of the "Golden Age" – the seventeenth century: a *Luncheon* by Velázquez, one of the country's finest masters, and two Murillos – *Boy with a Dog* and *Girl with a Basket of Fruit* (the latter is now in the Pushkin Museum in Moscow), purchased in Paris in 1772 at the sale of the collection of the Duc de Choiseul, one of Louis XV's ministers.

The growing collections needed to be housed somewhere. Between 1769 and 1775 Velten constructed long parallel picture galleries that connected the Northern and Southern Pavilions of the Hermitage. That proved insufficient and, in 1771–87, Velten added a new building alongside the Northern Pavilion – the Large or, as it is now known, Old Hermitage that accommodated the art collections.

From this point on, the original building was referred to as the Small Hermitage.

The Large Hermitage was still incomplete when, in 1783, the architect Giacomo Quarenghi (1744–1817) who had arrived from Italy, began work on new commissions from the Empress. Alongside the Large Hermitage he constructed the Raphael Loggias block and the Hermitage Theatre on either side of the Winter Canal.

The Raphael Loggias are a famous gallery in the Vatican. They were built in the sixteenth century by the architect Bramante, then painted by Raphael and his pupils. Between 1783 and 1785, Quarenghi constructed a building alongside the Winter Canal that contained a replica of the gallery in the Vatican produced from plans and measurements he himself had made before leaving Rome. In 1787–88 copies of Raphael's frescoes made on canvas in Rome by Christoph Unterberger and his assistants were attached to the walls and vaults of the gallery. Thus the Hermitage acquired a unique copy of a famous work of the Italian Renaissance.

On the other side of the Winter Canal, in 1783–89, Quarenghi constructed the Hermitage Theatre. This had been the site of Peter the Great's old Winter Palace in the early part of the century. Quarenghi produced a stage and auditorium and erected a superb white-columned façade on the Neva side, while preserving in his edifice the ground floor of Peter's palace. Velten linked the theatre to the Large Hermitage and Raphael Loggias with an exquisite arched bridge spanning the canal and carrying a covered walkway that incorporates the foyer of the theatre.

That is how Catherine's Large Hermitage was formed. Here, surrounded by priceless works of art, the Hermitage gatherings now took place, growing in scale and opulence as the years went on. They were now attended by the whole court, the family of the heir to the throne and diplomats – some 200 invited guests on occasion. The receptions usually began with a performance in the theatre, Catherine's beloved brainchild: she oversaw the productions and even wrote plays herself from time to time. The theatre staged operas, comedies and dramas, featuring some of the finest Russian and European actors. The musical directors were figures of European standing – Cimarosa, Galuppi, Paiziello. The evenings ended with dinner and a ball. The guests danced the polonaise through the halls of the Large Hermitage to the Small Hermitage, there the Empress danced the first minuet before withdrawing to her apartments, leaving her guests to enjoy themselves.

Catherine's private apartments were located in the Winter Palace, in a suite of rooms directly adjoining the Southern Pavilion of the Small Hermitage with windows overlooking Palace Square. Today it is hard to imagine what they looked like as the decoration has not survived. Many of the furnishings, however, are now in the Hermitage collection of applied art. Furniture made by the best French, German and English craftsmen, French tapestries, candelabra and chandeliers, mantelpiece clocks and table ornaments of gilded bronze created an atmosphere of refinement and regal splendour in the Empress's apartments. In the stores there are enormous quantities of porcelain from Meissen, Vienna, Berlin, and, particularly elegant and exquisite, Sèvres in France. For formal lunches and dinners the tables were laid with French and German silver. Close to the Throne Room, in Catherine's apartments, was the "Diamond Apartment" – a room where Catherine kept her valuables, jewellery made of gold, diamonds and precious stones, the legacy of earlier empresses, gifts and items commissioned from jewellers in Saint Petersburg and abroad. These pieces formed the basis of the Hermitage jewellery collection.

Nowadays the former Diamond Apartment contains paintings by the seventeenth-century French artist Nicolas Poussin. Many of these works, and those of other artist in the Hermitage's extremely rich collection of French art of the 1600s and 1700s were acquired in Catherine's time. Catherine's reign, the age of the Russian Enlightenment, saw the development of close ties with France and French culture. In enlightened circles there was a growing interest in the latest philosophical ideas emerging from France and in that nation's literature and art. That interest proceeded above all from the Empress. She corresponded with Voltaire and after the philosopher's death she bought his library and commissioned a statue of him seated in an armchair from the sculptor Jean-Antoine Houdon. Thanks to Diderot the Hermitage acquired the works of celebrated contemporary French artists. Diderot recommended the sculptor Etienne Maurice Falconet to Catherine for the creation of a monument to Peter the Great – the "Bronze Horseman" that was to become one of the finest adornments of Saint Petersburg. When he departed from Russia in 1778, Falconet left a number of sculptures that are now among the Hermitage masterpieces. On Diderot's advice Catherine bought Jean-Baptiste Greuze's painting *The Paralytic*, while Ivan Betskoi, the president of the Saint Petersburg Academy of Arts commissioned works from Chardin and Boucher that are also now in the Hermitage's French display.

The link with living, contemporary art was a distinctive feature of Catherine's Hermitage. As well as the paintings by French artists works were commissioned or bought in the studios of leading European artists of the day – Sir Joshua Reynolds, the president of the Royal Academy in London, Anton Raphael Mengs, the greatest master of German Classicism, and the noted female painter Angelica Kauffmann.

At one moment, when the Hermitage was just being formed, Diderot expressed his doubts: "It is impossible that a sufficient quantity of paintings will ever be accumulated in Russia to inspire a true taste for art." Yet, not without his own participation, by the end of Catherine the Great's reign her museum in the Hermitage was already reckoned one of the largest art collections in Europe. It numbered more than 4,000 paintings, over 7,000 drawings, almost 80,000 engravings, some 10,000 cameos and intaglios... That was the end result of the history of the Hermitage in the eighteenth century.

*The Great Hall
of the Northern Pavilion
of the Small Hermitage*
Drawing
BY J. FRIEDENREICH. 1840

The Oval Room
in the Old Hermitage
Drawing
BY J. FRIEDENREICH. 1839

16 (*opposite page, below*)
**The Hanging Garden
in the Small Hermitage**

The Northern and Southern
Pavilions were united by
two galleries with the still
surviving Hanging Garden
between them. This "miracle
of the world", supported by
powerful vaults, is lying at the
level of the first floor. During
its creation flower-beds were
arranged, with plants grown
in leaded tubs, walks were
laid out and marble sculptures
were placed around a fountain.
During the age of Catherine the
Great, a metal screen was put
around the Hanging Garden so
that in summer birds and
small animals could be let in.
In winter artificial hills for
sledge riding were made there.

15

VIGILIUS ERICHSEN (1722–1782)
*Portrait of Catherine the Great
in Front of a Mirror.* 1762
Oil on canvas
Acquired 1918 from the Romanov
Gallery in the Winter Palace

Vigilius Erichsen, a Danish
portrait painter, worked in
St Petersburg from 1757 to 1772.

14
**The Great Coronation Carriage.
First quarter of the 18th
century**
**The Gobelins Factory (?), Paris,
France** *(Room 193)*

This carriage was used for
coronation ceremonies which
were held in the Assumption
Cathedral of the Moscow
Kremlin. It was bought by Peter
the Great in Paris during his
travel abroad of 1716–17.
As witnessed by contemporaries,
it was in this carriage that
Catherine the Great reached the
Cathedral of the Assumption,
where her coronation ceremony
took place. During World War II
the carriage suffered serious
damage from the fragments of
a shell which hit the repository.
In 1991 its restoration was
completed and the formal
Baroque carriage can again be
seen in all its splendour.

17 ▲
The building of the Small Hermitage

The second building of the Hermitage complex, the Small Hermitage, connected by a passageway with the Winter Palace, was created by two well-known St Petersburg architects, Jean-Baptiste Vallin de la Mothe and Yury Velten. The Small Hermitage was built between 1764 and 1775. It must be emphasized that the honour to design the project belonged to Vallin de la Mothe. As for Velten, he headed for several years the construction of this building, located next to the official residence and intended for entertaining receptions and friendly meetings. The edifice consists of two pavilions. The Southern Pavilion overlooking Palace Square and Million-naya Street was originally intended for Count Grigory Orlov, a favourite of Catherine the Great. The classical façade of the Northern Pavilion which had several rooms inside, as well as a dining-room and the Orangery, created an expressive accent in the architectural appearance of the Hermitage complex.

18–20
The Peacock Clock
BY JAMES COX
Second half of the 18th century.
England
Details with a cock, owl
and mushroom-dial

Each of the figures inhabiting this miraculous realm created by the outstanding English master of mechanics has a distinctive character and manner of conduct. For example, the owl gazing at amazed viewers with a sense of dignity is slowly opening and closing her eyes, while the cock is crowing and flapping the wings.

21 ▶
The Peacock Clock
BY JAMES COX
Second half of the 18th century. England
(Room 204)

In the middle of the nineteenth century the interiors of the Northern Pavilion were completely refashioned. Instead of small rooms of the Catherine period there appeared the sparkling white-marble Pavilion Hall in the centre of which was placed the famous Peacock Clock produced in the eighteenth century by the celebrated English clock-maker James Cox. The clock, an acquisition of Prince Potemkin, arrived in St Petersburg dismantled and it took some efforts before the famous Russian master craftsman Ivan Kulibin assembled the mechanism and put it into operation in 1792. The clock was preserved in the Tauride Palace whence, after the owner's death, it entered the collection of Catherine the Great. The operation of the mechanism of the clock is accompanied by a gentle musical tune accompanied by the chime of bells. The exact time can be seen on the cap of the mushroom where the Roman figures indicate hours and the Arabic ones show minutes. When the mechanism located in the base of the tree and inside the birds is set into operation, each inhabitant of this elaborate, whimsical and nearly theatrical spectacle, as if with a wave of a magic wand, begins to move.

◄ 22

JOSHUA REYNOLDS (1723–1792)
Cupid Untying the Girdle
of Venus. 1788
Oil on canvas. 127.5 x 101 cm
Acquired 1792 from the collection
of Count Grigory Potemkin

The image of the goddess
of beauty and love created
by Reynolds is far from the
classical ideal. Contemporaries
saw in it a resemblance with
the well-known model Emma
Hart, who married the diplomat
Lord Hamilton and had
a romantic love affair with
Admiral Nelson. The canvas,
painted in a fluent and inspired
manner, can be classed as
a mythological painting with
a great degree of reservation.
The vibrant combinations of
saturated red, yellow and blue
shades recall Reynolds's interest
in colouristic developments
of Venetian painters.

23

JOSEPH WRIGHT OF DERBY
(1743–1797)
An Iron Forge Viewed from
Without. 1773
Oil on canvas. 105 x 140 cm. Acquired
late 1774 – early 1775 from the artist

Joseph Wright of Derby was
attracted by scenes in which man
is engaged in action or creation,
whoever it might be, a common
smith or a scholar in his laboratory.

◄ 24

JOSHUA REYNOLDS (1723–1792)
The Infant Hercules Strangling
the Serpents. 1786–88
Oil on canvas. 303 x 297 cm. Acquired
1789 from the artist

Reynolds derived a subject for this
painting from an ode by the Greek
poet Pindar. He found it perfectly
suitable for an allegory glorifying
the might of a young Russian
state. According to a myth, Hera,
the jealous wife of Zeus, the ruler
of the Olympian gods, made up her
mind to kill Hercules, son of Zeus
and the mortal woman Alcmene,
by sending into the crib of the
sleeping infant two giant snakes.
Hercules, who awoke from touches
of cold snake bodies, strangled
the serpents.

25
FRANS HALS
(BETWEEN 1581 AND 1585 – 1666)
*Portrait of a Young Man
with A Glove. Ca* 1650
Oil on canvas. 80 x 66.5 cm
Acquired from the J. E. Gotzkowsky
collection in Berlin

Boldly discarding the traditional idea of
a portrait as a faithful copy of the real model,
Hals created sharp, dynamic and memorable
images. Using powerful, expressive brushstrokes
and not indulging in elaboration of detail,
Hals records on the canvas his vision of
a contemporary character which is illustrative
of a new, independent and unrestrained Dutch
generation. As evidenced by an eighteenth-
century English sales catalogue, a young man
represented by Hals was a doctor.

26 ▶
ADRIAEN BROUWER (1605–1638)
Scene in a Tavern
Oil on panel. 25 x 33.5 cm
Acquired 1770 from the F. Tronchin
collection in Geneva

Brouwer was an unusual figure
in Flemish art. Contemporaries
described him as a careless idler,
drunkard and reveller, who "rarely
worked anywhere but in a tavern".
However, the brilliant talent of the
artist who studied in Holland
under Frans Hals, his working
capacity and his deep devotion
to art allow us to doubt the
descriptions given to the master
by his biographers.

27

JACOB VAN RUISDAEL (1628/29–1682)
The Marsh. Ca 1665
Oil on canvas. 72.5 x 99 cm. Acquired between 1763 and 1774

The Marsh is a masterpiece of not only Dutch art but of world
landscape painting as a whole. The image of nature created by the
artist has profound philosophical undertones and is characterized
by permanent changes, rejuvenation, dying and birth. Ruisdael's
landscape is permeated with majestic beauty and seems
to reflect lofty human feelings and aspirations.
But the grandeur and drama of the scene does not conceal a sense
of verisimilitude of the pictorial space enticing the viewer into
the depth of the painting where there is no marsh any more
and the dense masses of trees stand apart giving
a promise of light.

28
ANTOINE WATTEAU (1684–1721)
Savoyard with a Marmot. 1716
Oil on canvas. 40.5 x 32.5 cm
Acquired before 1774; formerly the Claude Audran collection in Paris

Antoine Watteau, a great French painter of the early eighteenth century, is represented
in the Hermitage by eight masterpieces. The artist was a forerunner of the Rococo style with its virtuosity and artistry,
but despite all the outward glitter of his mastery, Watteau's paintings are complicated and "closed" as was the personality
of the artist himself who died of tuberculosis at the age of thirty-seven in the prime
of his talent and at the peak of glory.

29

ANTOINE WATTEAU (1684–1721)
The Embarrassing Proposal. Ca 1716
Oil on canvas. 65 x 84.5 cm. Acquired 1769 from
the collection of Count Heinrich von Brühl in Dresden

Watteau is thought to have been the creator of
a special genre known as *fêtes galantes* of which
The Embarrassing Proposal is an illustrative
example.

30

FRANÇOIS BOUCHER (1703–1770)
Pastoral Scene
Oil on canvas. 61 x 75 cm (oval)
Acquired between 1763 and 1774

Boucher's paintings perhaps most fully epitomize
the lively spirit of the Rococo. The Hermitage
owns twenty paintings by this master. With an
equal dexterity he rendered a pastoral or mythological scene, a landscape or a portrait, he had
no problems with designing a stage set or a costume, a tapestry or a porcelain piece.

32 ▶

LUCAS CRANACH THE ELDER (1472–1553)
Portrait of a Lady. 1526
Oil on panel. 88.5 x 58.6 cm. Acquired before 1797

The Hermitage has four paintings by this
leading master of the German Renaissance. The young woman represented
in this magnificent painting is presumably
not a real sitter but rather an idealized
collective image, an ideal of beauty which
occurs in most of Cranach's works.
His various images of the Madonna and
Venus, real contemporary beauties and
imagined characters, with a typically
graceful oval of the face, elongated eyes
and golden hair, are always somewhat
mysterious and estranged, their glances
suggestive of some magic secret.

31

AMBROSIUS HOLBEIN (*CA* 1495– *CA* 1519)
Portrait of a Young Man. 1518
Oil on panel. 44 x 32.5 cm. Acquired between 1774 and 1783

Ambrosius Holbein, son and pupil of Hans Holbein the Elder, was active
together with his brother Hans Holbein the Younger. Ambrosius is known
as a master of portraiture, but he also painted religious subjects
and produced engravings illustrating works by Erasmus of Rotterdam.
The *Portrait of a Young Man* was evidently painted in Basel to which
the young Holbein brothers moved in 1515.

BARTOLOMÉ ESTEBAN MURILLO (1617–1682)
Boy with a Dog. 1650s
Oil on canvas. 74 x 60 cm. Acquired 1772 at a sale in Paris,
from the collection of the Duke de Choiseul

The *Boy with a Dog* is an example of the artist's early, "cold" style
named so because in this period cold tones often prevailed
in his colour scheme. Once the Hermitage possessed its companion
piece, *Girl with Fruit*, which is now in the Pushkin Museum
of Fine Arts in Moscow.

34
DIEGO VELÁZQUEZ (1599–1660)
Luncheon. Ca 1617–18
Oil on canvas. 108.5 x 102 cm. Acquired between 1763 and 1774
from an unknown collection

This painting belongs to the early period of the great Spanish
artist's career. At first sight, Velázquez depicts a real Spanish tavern
scene, but he invests the seemingly commonplace subject with
some additional meaning. The still life on the table –
a loaf, pomegranate and glass of wine – are Christian symbols
and the images of the boy, youth and old man might be related
to an idea of the three periods in human life.

33 ▲

BARTOLOMÉ ESTEBAN MURILLO
(1617–1682)
The Immaculate Conception
1670s
Oil on canvas. 195.6 x 145 cm
Acquired 1779 from the Walpole
collection at Houghton Hall, England

Paintings by Murillo, a celebrated artist of the seventeenth
century, the so-called Golden
Age of Spanish painting,
enjoyed enormous popularity
among art collectors.
The Hermitage possesses some
thirteen works by the famous
master representing various
periods of his creative career –
from the *estile frio* ("cold")
in the early years to the *estile
vaporoso* ("airy") in the later
years. *The Immaculate
Conception*, a virtuoso painting
in a light silver-blue gamut,
is a perfect example of
the artist's "airy" manner.
In the collection of Lord Walpole
at Houghton Hall in England
the painting was called
The Ascension of the Virgin,
but the white and blue colours
of her garments in this picture
suggest the theme of the
Immaculate Conception.

53 ▶
The Raphael Loggias. 1783–92
By Giacomo Quarenghi
(1744–1817)
Copy of Raphael's painting
in the Vatican Palace. 1780s
(Room 197)

The gallery designed by Giacomo
Quarenghi for Catherine the
Great, depicted copies of wall
paintings in the famous
Vatican gallery created by
Raphael and his assistants
in the early sixteenth century.
The gallery consists of thirteen
parts formed by semicircular
arches. The copies were made
by a group of artists under
the supervision of Christoph
Unterberger on canvases
directly in the Vatican.

◀ 52
Giorgione (Giorgio da Castelfranco)
(1478?–1510)
Judith. **Early 1500s**
Oil on canvas. 144 x 66.5 cm
Acquired 1772 from
the Pierre Crozat collection
in Paris

The first great Venetian painter, marking
the age of the High Renaissance, Giorgione lived
a short life — the celebrated master was about
thirty-two when he became a victim of smallpox
epidemic. Only about a dozen of Giorgione's
authentic works have reached us.
Judith is one of the Hermitage's masterpieces.
In the Crozat collection the canvas was
ascribed to Raphael.

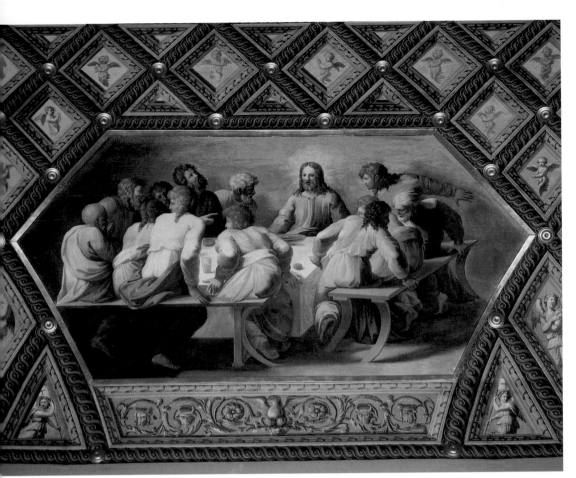

54
The Raphael Loggias. 1783–92
ARCHITECT GIACOMO QUARENGHI (1744–1817)
Copy of Raphael's painting
in the Vatican Palace. 1780s
The Last Supper
Detail of ceiling painting

The vaults of each part of the gallery
bear four painted Biblical
and Gospel scenes which received
the name of "Raphael's Bibles".
Gradually clear-cut classical pictorial
scenes on the ceiling unfold the entire
story narrated in the Old and New
Testament, from the creation of the world
to the Crucifixion of Christ.

56 ▶
The Raphael Loggias. 1783–92
ARCHITECT GIACOMO QUARENGHI (1744–1817)
Copy of Raphael's painting
in the Vatican Palace. 1780s
Scenes from the story
of Adam and Eva

55
The Raphael Loggias. 1783–92
ARCHITECT GIACOMO QUARENGHI (1744–1817)
Copy of Raphael's painting
in the Vatican Palace. 1780s
Detail of wall painting

The walls are decorated with
the so-called "grotesque" ornament –
a whimsical combination of fantastic
creatures, birds, fish, butterflies, flowers,
acanthus scrolls and human figures.
The austere symmetry in the placement
of the elements does not make
the ornament rigid because even
similar details are never
the same.

60 ▶▶
The southern façade
of the Winter Palace viewed
from Palace Square

57
The Hermitage Theatre. 1783–86
By Giacomo Quarenghi. (1744–1817)

A small theatre which had existed in the south-western
wing of the Winter Palace until the late 1770s, did not satisfy the
demands of Catherine the Great, and the court architect Quarenghi began
to construct a new building on the other side
of the Winter Canal. Later he would connect it with the Old Hermitage
by an arched bridge – a passageway which housed the foyer of the theatre.
The windows of the foyer afford a beautiful view of the Neva
and the Winter Canal.
The construction of the façade, the classical appearance of which has
survived to the present day, was completed in 1802.

58
The Hermitage Theatre. 1783–86
BY GIACOMO QUARENGHI (1744–1817)
The Auditorium

The Hermitage Theatre had an unusual
appearance. Instead of common richly adorned
boxes and seats rising in galleries, Quarenghi
designed the auditorium like an amphitheatre
with semicircular rows of seats divided
by descending staircases. As the architect
commented, "in this theatre any etiquette is
discarded, there are no special seats and one can
choose any place he or she likes".
The columns and walls are covered with
artificial marble; in the niches are placed the
statues of the Muses making the interior more
expressive; the huge, deep stage is decorated
with a marvellous curtain.

59
Portrait of the Architect
Giacomo Quarenghi
BY D. POLLY. 1810s
The Bergamo Municipal Office, Italy

Giacomo Quarenghi (1744–1817)
was born near Bergamo in Italy.
His grandfather and father
were artists. On 1 September
1779 Quarenghi signed a
contract for three years with
a representative of the Russian
authorities. But he stayed in
Russia, with short intervals, for
thirty-five years, until his death
and created in St Petersburg
a number of architectural
masterpieces. He entered the
history of culture as an eminent
exponent of austere Classicism
in Russian architecture.

61 ▼

Commode. 1765–70
BY DAVID ROENTGEN (1743–1808)
AND ABRAHAM ROENTGEN
France
Wood, with marquetry decoration
and bronze mounts

Marquetry is a process of inlay decoration with
thin pieces of coloured woods. It was frequently
used to decorate furniture in the Rococo period.

63 ▶

Mantel clock. 1780s
AFTER THE MODEL
BY JEAN ANTOINE HOUDON
Ormolu, marble
Acquired after the 1917 Revolution

This clock on a marble stand
is a miniature version
of an elaborate architectural
structure: two caryatids
flanking the dial support
a panel bearing two bronze
incense-burners; a round
pedestal set in the centre of
the composition and encircled
with the figures of doves
is completed by a sculptural
group of kissing lovers.
The dial bears the name
of the clock-maker: *H. Burret
à Paris*.

62

Bureau. 1780s
BY DAVID ROENTGEN
(1743–1808)
Wood and bronze
(Room 289)

David Roentgen, a well-known
master craftsman, cabinet-
maker to the King of France,
supplied his works to many
European courts including that
of Russia. Bureaux produced
in his workshop often contain
all kinds of secrets, ingenious
mechanisms and musical
caskets.

64
Service with cameos. 1778–79
Sèvres, France
Porcelain

This festive service produced at the Sèvres Porcelain Factory
for Catherine the Great comprises 800 items.
The service was embellished with representations of ancient
cameos alternating with plant ornaments.
The flower garlands form the Empress's monogram.
During the fire of 1837 about 160 pieces
from this service were stolen and some ten years
later appeared at a sale in London.
Thanks to the efforts
of Russian diplomats they were returned to Russia.
Now the Hermitage collection contains
688 items.

65

**Tobacco-box with a medal commemorating
the twentieth anniversary of Catherine
the Great's ascension to the throne
on its cover. 1774**
By Jean-Pierre Ador (1724–1784)
Gold

There were thirty pieces of this kind.
They were intended as gifts to participants in
the coup which resulted in the death of Peter III,
Catherine's husband, and her ascension
to the throne.

66
The Green Frog Service. 1773–74
By Josiah Wedgwood (1730–1795)
England
Creamware

The service was commissioned by Catherine the Great from Wedgwood for a roadside palace built at the southern end of St Petersburg on the way to Peterhof and Tsarskoye Selo (it was later named the Chesme Palace). The locality was known as Kekerikeksen, which meant "a frog marsh" in Finnish, hence the crest of the service – a green frog emblazoned on a shield. The service was intended for fifty eaters and included dinner (680 items decorated with garlands of oak leaves) and dessert (264 items framed with a garland of ivy). Each item of the service was decorated with a real, topographically faithful view of Great Britain painted in dark purple against a cream-coloured background.

67
Portrait of Elizabeth I
of England
By Julien de Fontenay (?)
Ca 1685. England
Sardonyx. 5.1 x 3.7 cm
Acquired 1787 from the collection
of the Duc d'Orleans

68 ▶
**Snuff-box
with a representation
of the dog Lisette,
Catherine the Great's pet**
By Johann-Gottlieb Scharff
1770s (?)
Gold, enamel colours, emeralds
and diamonds

The snuff-box belonged
to Catherine the Great or
to somebody from her closest
associates.

69
**Badge of distinction with
the monogram of Catherine
the Great. Second half
of the 18th century**
Gold and diamonds

Such insignia were worn
by the ladies-in-waiting
to Catherine the Great.

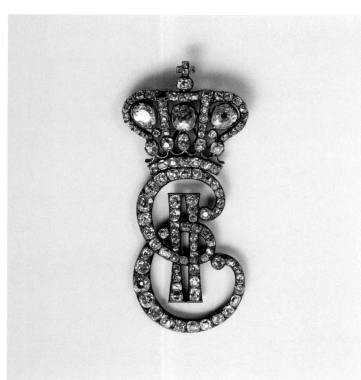

70

LOUIS LE NAIN (1593–1648)
The Milkwoman's Family. 1640s
Oil on canvas. 51 x 59 cm
Acquired between 1763 and 1774

This painting is a masterpiece by the celebrated Louis Le Nain,
an artist who belonged to the circle of the so-called
"painters of the real world".
The subject matter of the canvas, an example of the "peasant
genre", is devoid of any narrative or entertaining details.
The peasant family, depicted against the huge greyish-blue sky,
evokes a feeling of dignity and self-reliance.
The austere and thought-out composition which distinguishes
this modest genre painting exemplifies the best features
of elevated French Classicism in the seventeenth century.

71
NICOLAS POUSSIN (1594–1665)
Tancred and Erminia. 1630s
Oil on canvas. 98.5 x 146.5 cm
Acquired 1772 from the collection of the artist
Jacque André-Joseph Aved in Paris

Poussin, the great creator of French Classicism, declared that
the picture begins with a subject which must have a noble character.
His *Tancred and Erminia* is based on the poem *Jerusalem Delivered*
by Torquato Tasso, a famous Italian Renaissance poet.
The scene chosen by the artist deals with the love of a pagan
woman, Erminia, who knew the secrets of magic,
to a noble knight, the crusader Tancred.
The knight, eager to make heroic feats for his holy faith,
set out for the Crusade. On learning that Tancred was mortally
wounded in a battle with the giant Organt,
Erminia discovered the dying knight on the battlefield
and saved him. She cut off her hair which possessed magic power
to bind his wounds, but on doing this for the sake of love,
Erminia lost her magic gift for ever.

72
Nicolas Poussin (1594–1665)
Satyr and Bacchante, 1630s
Oil on canvas. 72 x 56 cm
Acquired 1772 from
the Pierre Crozat collection in Paris

The theme of bacchanalia — ancient festivals
of Bacchus, the god of wine, were a recurrent source
of inspiration for Poussin in the 1630s when he devoted
to it a number of his works in the so-called Venetian
cycle permeated with a truly heathen joy of life.
The painting *Satyr and Bacchante* is likely to have been
one of his numerous studies on this subject.

73
NICOLAS POUSSIN (1594–1665)
Landscape with Polythemus. 1640s
Oil on canvas. 150 x 199 cm
Acquired 1772 from the Marquise
de Conflant collection in Paris

In the late 1640s Poussin created a series of majestic landscapes
devoted to the harmonious unity of eternal Nature
and all the creatures inhabiting it.
The earth, trees, mountains,
gods, people, nymphs and satyrs seem to listen,
holding their breath, to the magic sounds of a pipe played by
the cyclop Polyphemus. Seated on a rock, he is pouring out his
sad feelings connected with his unrequited love
to the beautiful sea-nymph Galatea.

74
CLAUDE GELLÉE, CALLED LORRAIN (1600–1682)
Morning in the Harbour. 1640s
Oil on canvas. 74 x 97 cm
Acquired 1781 from
the Count de Boudoin collection in Paris

Paintings by Lorrain who came to Italy as a youth and spent his whole life there, served as a standard of an elevated classical landscape based on the study of real Italian nature for many generations of French painters.
The special light effects characteristic of the Italian countryside in different times of day are captured by Lorrain with their subtle variations in his series of paintings called *Morning, Noon, Evening* and *Night*.

75
The suite of rooms devoted to French art of the 18th century
BY ALEXANDER BRIULLOV (1798–1876)
(Rooms 272–289)

This suite of rooms was originally designed by the architect Rastrelli as the living apartments of Empress Elizabeth but after her death the same architect refashioned it for the next Emperor, Peter III.
After the coup, when Catherine the Great ascended the throne, Vallin de la Mothe completely redesigned the interiors of the suite in the late 1760s to meet the tastes of the new Empress of Russia. At the end of the 1790s the design of these rooms was altered again, this time by Giacomo Quarenghi. In 1818 Carlo Rossi refashioned the suite for the important guest, William Frederick II of Prussia. After the fire of 1837 the decoration of the rooms underwent drastical alterations by the architect Alexander Briullov.
The suite had no permanent owner and it began to be named the Second Reserve Apartments.

The
HERMITAGE

The Imperial Museum: The 19th Century

85

Panoramic view of Palace Square and the centre of the city from the roof of the Winter Palace, with the Angel crowning the Alexander Column

The powerful granite column installed by the architect Auguste de Montferrand in the centre of Palace Square to commemorate the victory of the Russian army in the war against Napoleon Bonaparte, was named after the victorious Emperor of Russia, Alexander I. The column is the focus of the entire Palace Square perfectly balanced with the proportions of the Winter Palace and the General Staff building shaping the square. The column's dimensions are impressive: the weight of the giant hewn monolith amounts to about 704 tonnes and its overall length is 47.5 metres – it is the tallest triumphal column in the world. The ceremony of unveiling the column was held in 1834.

84

BORIS ORLOVSKY (1796–1837)

Statue of the Angel crowning the Alexander Column

The sculptor Boris Orlovsky, who produced the Angel with a cross crowning the Alexander Column, was the son of a serf peasant. He revealed a talent for modelling in his childhood and was sent to Moscow for training under the marble-worker S. Tampioni. In 1822 he enrolled at the Academy of Arts in St Petersburg and was later sent, with some other students, for further training to Italy where he spent five years. On his return to St Petersburg in 1829 he received many commissions for monumental sculpture intended as decorations of the capital's architectural ensembles. The architect Montferrand offered him to create the figure of an Angel for the Alexander Column which was being erected in the centre of Palace Square. The inauguration of the monument took place in 1834.

86
The Hall of Peter the Great
BY AUGUSTE DE MONTFERRAND (1786–1858)
Detail of vault decoration

The compositional focus of the hall built in 1833 is the niche having
a semicircular vault embellished with elements of the imperial attributes –
crossed Latin monograms of Peter the Great,
double-headed eagles
and crowns.

The Hall of Peter the Great
BY AUGUSTE DE MONTFERRAND (1786–1858)
(Room 194)

The Hall of Peter the Great or the Small Throne Room was reconstructed by Vasily Stasov after the fire of 1837 to its former appearance. The hall is dedicated to the memory of Peter the Great. Its walls are lined with crimson silver-embroidered velvet brought from Lyons. Above, on the side walls, are decorative paintings representing Peter the Great against the background of the battles of the Northern War – the Battle of Poltava and the Battle of Lesnaya – executed by the artists Barnaba Medici and Pietro Scotti.

93
The 1812 War Gallery
By Carlo Rossi (1775–1849)
(Room 197)

This gallery adjoining the main interior of the Winter Palace, the St George Hall, is a memorial of Russian martial glory. It houses 332 portraits of generals, participants in the war against Napoleon in 1812–14. They were painted by the English portrait painter Georg Dawe (1789–1829) in 1819–28. The gallery was illuminated through glazed openings in the vaults supporting the arches. The fire of 1837 destroyed the interior, but most of the portraits were saved and did not suffer any serious damage. After the fire Stasov restored the gallery practically to its former appearance.

94
Franz Krüger (1797–1857)
Equestrian Portrait of Emperor Alexander I. 1837
Oil on canvas. 484 x 344 cm. Painted for the 1812 War Gallery

The German artist Franz Krüger was the favourite painter of formal portraits of Nicholas I and Russian officers of the highest rank. Portrait of Alexander I was painted by the artist to replace the formal portrait of the Emperor by Dawe lost in the fire. In 1837, after the restoration of the hall was completed, the portrait was hung, to replace Dawe's lost work, in the niche of the end wall under the velvet canopy.

99
The St George Hall
By Vasily Stasov (1769–1848)

The St George Hall,
or the Great Throne Room,
is one of the best state halls
in the Winter Palace,
a magnificent example of
nineteenth-century Russian
Classicism. Its walls are
covered with tiles of white
Carrara marble; the same
marble is used for the slender
fluted columns with bronze
Corinthian capitals.
The heavy coffered copper
ceiling suspended from iron
structures was decorated with
a gilded bronze ornament,
the pattern of which repeats,
in a mirror-like manner,
in the design of the luxurious
parquet floor inlaid with
sixteen kinds of precious
wood. Opposite the entrance,
over the throne place,
is situated a marble relief
representing St George,
the patron of the Russian
Tsar's family.

The Malachite Drawing-Room
By Alexander Briullov (1798–1876)
Watercolour by Konstantin Ukhtomsky
1865

101 ▶
The Malachite Drawing-Room
By Alexander Briullov (1798–1876)
(Room 189)

The apartments of Nicholas I's wife, Empress Alexandra
Fiodorovna, are marked by a great luxury. From 1830s, after huge
deposits of malachite were found at the Demidovs' mines in the
Urals, this valuable, rarely beautiful green stone began to be used
for the decoration of luxurious St Petersburg interiors.
The Malachite Room, redesigned after the fire of 1837 by
Alexander Briullov, strikes by an effective if somewhat ponderous
combination of an abundant gilding with a bright green
of numerous malachite details and a white of artificial marble
of the walls and crimson upholstery of gilded furniture.
One wall in the Drawing-Room is decorated with a painting over
a white stucco, featuring allegorical figures personifying Night,
Day and Poetry, a work by Antonio Vighi.

102
**Details of the decoration
of the Malachite Room.
Malachite objects**

The columns and fireplaces as well
as numerous vases, table-tops and smaller
objects displayed in the showcases
of the Malachite Room are executed
in the complex technique known
as Russian mosaic work: thin plaques
of the stone were glued to the base,
the joints were filled with malachite powder
and then the surface
was polished.

104 ▶
The Malachite Drawing-Room
By Alexander Briullov
(1798–1876)
(Room 189)

103
Vase. 1840s
Malachite and ormolu. The Lapidary Works, Peterhof

The unique technique of malachite treatment
was evolved by Russian craftsmen and that is
why it is called Russian mosaic work. Beginning
his work with a piece of malachite, a craftsman
did not know what kind of pattern is inside the
stone. Only his natural feeling and his
experience handed over from one generation
to another enabled him to reveal the beauty
of ornament and the specific chromatic qualities
of this semiprecious stone mined in the Urals.
When creating malachite vases, artists usually
made use of traditional forms known since
Classical Antiquity.

105
The Pompeian Dining-Room
Watercolour by Konstantin Ukhtomsky. 1864
The interior has not survived

Architect Alexander Briullov decorated the walls of the Small
or Pompeian Dining-Room in the living apartments of Nicholas
I's wife with variations on the subjects of Pompeian frescoes –
in the 1820s he took part in excavations at Pompeii.
This small room was covered with a flat metal ceiling
decorated with an exquisite ornament, and the coloured
parquet floor with an elaborate geometrical pattern completed
the decor.

106
Bathroom in the Moorish Style
Watercolour by Konstantin Ukhtomsky. 1864
The interior has not survived

When decorating the Bathroom for the Empress, Architect Alexander
Briullov demonstrated a deep knowledge of Eastern architecture,
primarily of the well-known palace-citadel Alhambra, the residence of the
rulers of the Granada Emirate. He succeeded in subtly reproducing the
specific features of Moorish-Spanish architecture.
The colour gamut of the bathroom is also typical for interiors
of the Alhambra palace.

107 ▶
The October Staircase
By Auguste de Montferrand (1786–1858)

The staircase was decorated by Auguste
de Montferrand in the early 1830s and
was restored by Alexander Briullov after the fire
without radical alterations.
Earlier it had been called "Her Majesty's
Staircase" for it led to the living apartments
of the Dowager Empress Maria Fiodorovna,
wife of Paul I,
and later Empress Maria Alexandrovna.
During the storming of the Winter Palace
in the night of 25 to 26 October 1917
(7 to 8 November New Style),
revolutionary soldiers and sailors used the
staircase to arrest the Provisional Government,
hence its name – the October Staircase.

109 ▶
The White Hall
By Alexander Briullov
(1798–1876)
(Room 289)

The so-called New Apartments of the heir, the future Emperor Alexander II, included the rooms of his consort, Maria Alexandrovna. The main room in this half was the festive White Hall. The decor of this magnificent interior illuminated by two rows of windows included representations of war trophies, allegorical figures and bas-reliefs showing mythological subjects.

108
The Green Dining-Room. 1850
By Andrei Stakenschneider (1802–1865)
(Room 308)

Next to the Golden Drawing-Room, within the living apartments
of Empress Maria Alexandrovna, was built a dining-room designed in the
Rococo style with a large quantity of stuccowork, painted insets
and mirrors. Since the dining-room had no windows, in the daytime
the room was illuminated through an oval lantern in the ceiling.
The walls were turned into festive panels with mirrors.
The fireplace near the northern wall is executed of precious kind of marble
named *porto-venera*. The furniture in the Dining-Room was upholstered
with green Gobelin fabric and the dining table covered
with a green table-cloth.

The Golden Drawing-Room
BY ALEXANDER BRIULLOV (1798–1876)
(Room 304)

Another element of decor was carved, entirely gilded doors
with carved ornaments. In the 1860s and 1870s the walls
of the drawing-room were covered with gilding throughout.
Today the Golden Drawing-Room houses the collection of articles
made of multilayered semiprecious carved stones – cameos
and intaglios of cornelian, agate, chalcedony,
amethyst and onyx – executed by skilful
Western European masters.
This is one of the largest collections of this kind in Europe.
It was begun by Catherine the Great who explained
her passion for stones by a special
"cameo disease".

110
The Golden Drawing-Room
BY ALEXANDER BRIULLOV
(1798–1876)
Detail of ceiling decoration

The Golden Drawing-Room was conceived by
Briullov as an interior contrasting with the adjacent
White Hall. In the luxury of its decor it was to
echo the main drawing-room of Nicholas I's wife,
the Malachite Room, which in the nineteenth
century was also known as the Golden Room.
Originally the walls and the vault were lined
with white artificial marble and gilding was used
to single out a thin moulded ornament.

111
The Golden Drawing-Room
BY ALEXANDER BRIULLOV (1798–1876)
Fireplace

The furniture in the Golden Drawing-Room
of Empress Maria Alexandrovna was entirely
gilded and the panels were painted in imitation
of lapis-lazuli. The decor of the hall was added
by a marble fireplace with a bas-relief and
mosaic landscape. In front of the fireplace stood
a screen of ruby-coloured glass defending from
sparkles and heat. The intense red colour was
achieved by adding gold into melted glass.

118 ▶

FRANCISCO DE ZURBARÁN
(1598–1664)
The Girlhood of the Madonna
Ca 1660
Oil on canvas . 73.5 x 53.5 cm
Acquired 1814 from the Baron
de Coesevelt collection in Amsterdam

The Girlhood of the Madonna
was one of Zurbarán's
favourite subjects. The Virgin
Mary is shown seated
on a small children's chair,
her hands are put on a small
pillow specially intended for
praying and her dress is
embroidered with an elegant
gilded pattern. Like in his
other works on religious
subjects, the master succeeded
to blend a restraint and
complete aloofness from all
earthly things with expressive,
distinctly Spanish features
of life.

117
DIEGO VELÁZQUEZ (1599–1660)
Portrait of Count-Duke of Olivares. Ca 1640
Oil on canvas . 67 x 54.5 cm
Acquired 1814 from the Baron de Coesevelt collection in Amsterdam

Don Gaspar de Guzmán, Count of Olivares, Duke of San Lucár,
became the mighty Prime-Minister since the moment
when the sixteen-year-old Philip IV had ascended the throne.
The clever. sly, well-educated and energetic Olivares concentrated
all power in his hands. It was thanks to him that the young
Velázquez received the position of court painter. The portrait, very
simple and austere in composition, reflects the complicated,
tragically contradictory character of the factual ruler of Spain who
would have to spend the end of his life in exile.

119
ANTONIO PEREDA (1608–1678)
Still Life. 1652
Oil on canvas. 80 x 94 cm
Acquired 1814 from the Baron de Coesevelt
collection in Amsterdam

120
JUAN PANTOJA DE LA CRUZ
(1553–1608)
*Portrait of Diego
de Villamayor.* 1605
Oil on canvas. 89 x 71 cm
Acquired 1814 from the
Baron de Coesevelt collection
in Amsterdam

Juan Pantoja de la Cruz, court
painter to the Kings Philip II
and Philip III, was active
in Madrid and at the royal
residence El Escorial.
Diego de Villamayor belonged
to the celebrated aristocratic
family – its origins went
as far back as the eleventh
century. The Order of Alcantara
which could be worn only
by the selected few suggests
the noble origin of the
seventeen-year-old grandee.

Pereda seems to carefully touch every object in his still life
delighting in the transparency of glass, density
and brightness of painted crockery,
the glitter of a metal vessel for boiling coffee,
comparing their textures with biscuits and cheese
in the foreground which introduce a sense
of invisible human presence into the realm
of "dead nature".

DI DAC⁵ V⁵ MO⁵
·ÆTATIS SVÆ·

·17·ANNO·1609

Ju⁰ Pantoja dela
✝ Faciebat
1609

122 ▶

**The State Staircase
of the New Hermitage
By Leo von Klenze
(1784–1864)**

The Bavarian architect Leo von Klenze, the designer of the famous Pinakothek in Munich, designed the first Russia's museum building which became known as the New Hermitage. The unique character of the architect's concept lies in its unity, for Klenze presented not only his architectural project but also sketches of painted decorations of the interiors as well as of sculpture, furniture, museum showcases and stands. The ground floor was intended for displaying the collection of sculpture. The wide staircase leading to the first floor, where the collection of painting was displayed, was divided into three flights. The white polished marble steps, the perfectly polished yellow stucco of the walls effectively contrasted with the austere vestibule with sixteen columns of Finnish granite, seeming even somewhat dim in comparison with the well-lit staircase. The twenty grey tall columns of Serdobolye granite supporting the roof beams add and complete the architectural composition, rhythmically slender and exquisite in colour.

121
Resting Satyr (right)
**First half of the 4th century B.C.
Roman copy from the original by Praxiteles**
Marble

Nicholas I, who commissioned the Bavarian architect Leo von Klenze
to design the first Russian public museum, began to intensely replenish
the Hermitage collection with works which would be placed
in the new repository. He did this in different ways. Since the collection
of ancient sculpture in the Hermitage was only taking shape.
Nicholas I received in 1851 from the Pope several
ancient statues including this *Resting Satyr*, in exchange for a plot
of land on Palatine Hill in Rome.

129 ▶
Fragment of a statue of
an army leader. 1st century B.C.
Marble. Acquired 1851 from
the A. Demidov collection

◀ 128
Statue: *Jupiter*
1st century B.C.
Marble, tinted plaster.
Acquired 1861 from the Marquise
de Campana collection in Paris

The statue was found in
the nineteenth century during
excavations of an ancient
temple in the environs of Rome
and goes back to the ancient
masterpiece by the great
sculptor Phidias which has
not survived. The great Greek
master active in the fifth
century B.C. created a statue
of Zeus in the chryselephantine
technique — as a combination
of ivory and gold.
The Hermitage statue once had
been produced by the acrolithic
method which combined
marble for the extremities and
gilded wood for the rest of the
figure. The wooden parts have
not survived and were replaced
by tinted plaster.

130
Bust of Empress Salonina
Mid-3rd century A.D.
Marble
Acquired 1787 from
the D. Lyde Browne collection

Julia Cornelia Salonina,
wife of Emperor Gallenius
is represented as Venus
the Primogenitor.

131
Head of Antinous
Second quarter of the 2nd century A.D.
Marble

Antinous, a youth of an extraordinary beauty,
was a favourite of the Roman Emperor Hadrian
(117–138). After he had drowned in the Nile,
the grief of the Emperor knew no bounds
and he decided to enroll Antinous among the
gods. Marble portraits of the youth could be seen
in many cities of the Roman Empire.

132
The Kolyvan Vase. 1847
The Kolyvan Lapidary Works, Altai Mountains
Revniukha jasper. *(Room 128)*

This vase, one of the most remarkable examples of
Russian stone-carving, was commissioned specially
as a decoration for a certain room on the first floor
of the New Hermitage. But weighing some nineteen
tonnes it proved to be too heavy for the intended
place and was therefore installed on the ground
floor in a room devoted to Classical Antiquity.
The immense vase, produced by stone-cutters at the
lapidary works in the Altai Mountains, took twelve
years to complete. It is more than 2.5 metres high
and its bowl, hewn from a single block of stone,
is about five metres in diameter. The vase is made up
of five collapsible monolithic parts.

133 ▶
The Hall of Twenty Columns
By Leo von Klenze (1784–1864)
(Room 130)

This hall was designed specially for an exhibition
of ancient painted vases. It is natural that Klenze,
who was well versed in classical art,
used ancient motifs in the decor of the interior.
The two rows of granite columns support the beams
of the ceiling divided into squares reminiscent
of the articulation of Greek temples.
In the upper part of the walls are twelve
compositions representing vase paintings unfolded,
as it were, on the surface.
The hall is the only example of the museum interior
of the mid-nineteenth century surviving
in its original appearance.

138
**The upper landing
of the State Staircase
in the New Hermitage
By Leo von Klenze (1784–1864)**

The upper landing of the New Hermitage
staircase leads to the rooms
of the first floor designed specially
to display painting.
Over the entrance to the rooms is a plaque
with the inscription in Russian and Latin:
"Built by Emperor Nicholas I in 1852."

139
**Western European Sculpture
of the 19th Century at the landing
of the State Staircase
in the New Hermitage**

In order to augment the Hermitage collection of sculpture,
Nicholas I made several travels to Italy.
There, after his visits to the studios of well-known sculptors
of different nationalities living in Rome, he bought a number of
marble statues which were used to decorate the staircase landing
in the new imperial museum in St Petersburg.
The assembled collection consisted of decorative sculptures by the
then fashionable Neo-Classical masters, the Italians Lorenzo
Bartolini, Giovanni Dupré and Luigi Bienaimé and the Germans
Emil Wolff, Christian Rauch and Wilhelm von Schadow.

142 ▶

**The Gallery of the History
of Ancient Painting**
By Leo von Klenze (1784–1864)
(Room 241)

According to Klenze's concept, the gallery
was to give an idea of the development
of ancient painting and of several extinct
paintings by great ancient artists.
The architect chose
86 subjects and entrusted the artist
Georg Hiltensperger with the task of creating
decorative panels for the gallery's walls.
The paintings are produced on copper plates
in wax colours in imitation of encaustics,
an ancient technique of painting.
The gallery houses the collection of sculptures
by major representatives of Neo-Classicism
of the eighteenth and nineteenth
centuries – Antonio Canova
and Bertel Thorvaldsen.

◀ 140

The Gallery of the History of Ancient Painting
Malachite vase. 19th century
The Lapidary Works, Yekaterinburg

141 ▶

Antonio Canova (1757–1822)
Cupid and Psyche. 1796
Marble. Acquired 1926 from
the Prince Yusupov collection
Detail

Canova, a fine master of Neo-Classicism,
interprets the final episode of an ancient legend
about Cupid and his love for Psyche.
Venus, Cupid's mother, made up her mind to kill
the beautiful young girl by ordering her to bring
back from the Underworld kingdom of Hades
a jug of beauty ointment.
Psyche was not allowed to open the cover,
but she, giving way to curiosity, could not help
doing so and instantly fell overcome
with a deathlike sleep which was put inside
instead of the beauty ointment.

◀ 143
ANTONIO CANOVA (1757–1822)
Hebe
Marble. Acquired 1815 from the Joséphine
de Beauharnais collection

One of Canova's most famous works, the statue
of Hebe, the goddess of youth, exists
in four copies. According to legend, Hebe was
the official cupbearer of the gods.
The sculptor depicted the goddess with
a jug goblet in her hands, quickly sliding
as it were, over a cloud descending
from Mount Olympus.

144
JOHN GIBSON (1790–1866)
Cupid the Shepherd
Marble

The English Neo-Classicist sculptor John Gibson
arrived in Rome in 1817 with a recommendation
letter to Antonio Canova and spent three years
in his workshop. His works enjoyed great
popularity with his compatriots and travellers
from other countries who liked to visit his studio
in Rome and make commissions from the
fashionable sculptor. In 1836 Gibson became
a member of the Royal Academy in London, but
he still remained in Italy throughout his lifetime.

145
ANTONIO CANOVA
(1757–1822)
The Three Graces. 1813
Marble. Acquired 1901
from the Duke
of Leuchtenberg collection

The famous sculptural group
The Three Graces was
commissioned to Canova
by Joséphine de Beauharnais,
but the commissioner died
in 1814, never seeing the
masterpiece of the sculptor
whom he adored. It was
Joséphine's son, Eugène
de Beauharnais, who received
the sculpture. The artist's
contemporaries admired
the images of the three graces
believing that Canova has
found and expressed the new
ideal of beauty in them.
The group was purchased
for the Hermitage collection
by Nicholas II.

146
The Large Italian Skylight
By Leo von Klenze
(1784–1864)
(Room 238)

The three central halls
of the first floor intended
for the exhibition of Western
European painting
(today it houses works by
Italian painters of the
seventeenth and eighteenth
centuries and the collection
of Spanish painting) were
called "Skylights" for the
special top lighting from above
through glass ceilings. In this
way Klenze freed for hanging
pictures the entire surface
of the walls. The halls are
decorated with gilded
moulding and painting.
The furniture designed after
a drawing by Klenze, perfectly
matches the red colour of
the walls and decorative vases,
torchères and table-tops of
semiprecious stones.

152 ▶

151
ROGIER VAN DER WEYDEN (ROGIER DE LA PASTURE)
(CA 1400–1464)
St Luke Drawing the Virgin. Mid-15th century
Oil on canvas, transferred from a panel. 102.5 x 108.5 cm
Acquired 1850 from the collection of William II of the Netherlands in The Hague,
and in 1884 from the art dealer Antoine Baer in St Petersburg

Legend has it that the great Dutch painter produced this painting for
the chapel of Brussels painters. Today, several version of this composition
can be found in various museums of the world and there is a controversy
as to which of them is the original. All of them are likely to be perfectly done
copies produced in the artist's studio. Nevertheless the Hermitage version
is a superb example of Netherlandish art.
Once the picture had been cut into two parts one of which was purchased
for the Hermitage in The Hague. Thirty years later another half was brought
to St Petersburg by a Parisian art dealer. The two halves were united,
butthe upper part of the composition has been lost.

The Tent-Roof Hall
BY LEO VON KLENZE (1784–1864)
(Room 249)

This room which now houses
the collection of seventeenth-
century Dutch painting received
its name for a special form˙
of its gable roof reminiscent
of a tent.
The small sections of the coffered
ceiling are adorned with painted
ornaments.

**The Room of Flemish Decorative Painting
of the 17th Century**
By Leo von Klenze (1784–1864)
(Room 245)

In the nineteenth century the room was used to display
paintings of the Russian school. Today it houses large-
scale paintings by major Flemish artists – Frans Snyders,
Paul de Voos and Jacob Jordaens as well as genre paintings
by David Teniers the Younger, Adriaen Brouwer and others.

157
Frans Snyders (1579–1657)
Fruit Shop. **Between 1618 and 1621**
Oil on canvas. 206 x 342 cm
Acquired 1779 from the Lord Walpole collection
at Houghton Hall, England

The still life in the series of shops painted by Snyders has been
raised to the height of truly large-scale art in which the main
role is played by objects, while human figures occupy
but an auxiliary place being merely a staffage.
It is not a mere chance that Snyders commonly entrusted
the painting of figures to his pupils.

◀ **158**
DAVID TENIERS THE YOUNGER
(1610–1690)
Peasant Wedding. 1650
Oil on canvas. 82 x 108 cm
Acquired 1767 at the auction
of the Jean de Jullienne
collection in Paris

David Teniers the Younger was
a major Flemish genre painter,
but his works are not
characterized by the
monumentality of forms
typical of Flemish painting.
He was extremely prolific and
painted hundreds of pictures
during his career.
Teniers told about them:
"It is necessary to build
a gallery two *lieues* long
to accommodate my paintings."
The characters of his *Peasant
Wedding* look like skilfully
garbed puppets united
by the artist as a dexterous
director in a theatrical
performance.

◄ 159
PAUL DE VOOS (1596–1678)
Hunting a Leopard. Mid-17th century
Oil on canvas. 205 x 345 cm
Acquired 1769 from the Heinrich von Brühl
collection in Dresden

Paul de Voos specialized in the depiction
of animals. Five large *Hunts* owned
by the Hermitage once presumably belonged
to the same series. Decorative paintings
by this master, highly prized in Flanders
and Spain, were used for the embellishment
of hunting lodges and suburban castles
of the nobility.

160
JACOB JORDAENS (1593–1678)
The Bean King. Ca 1638
Oil on canvas. 157 x 211 cm. Acquired 1922
from the Museum of the
Academy of Arts in Petrograd

The subject of the painting is a traditional
Netherlandish feast of the Three Kings, or the Three
Magi, celebrated on 6 January in honour
of the Magi who came to present gifts to the Infant
Christ. During that day pies were baked
in every home, with a bean put inside of one of them.
The one who would find the bean in his pie,
was honoured as the "king" of the holiday.
The painting features the moment
when everybody is lifting his or her goblet in honour
of the good-natured and grey-haired old man
who became the "bean king".

◀ 161
The Anthony van Dyck Room
BY LEO VON KLENZE
(1784–1864)
(Room 246)

The room houses twenty-four
paintings by the celebrated
Flemish portrait painter
Anthony van Dyck.

162 ▶
ANTHONY VAN DYCK
(1599–1641)
Self-Portrait
Late 1620s – early 1630s
Oil on canvas. 116.5 x 93.5 cm
Acquired 1772 from the collection
of Pierre Crozat in Paris

The refinement and elegance characteristic
of Van Dyck's mature period were implemented in his self-portrait
executed in Antwerp after his return from Italy.
Van Dyck certainly idealizes his image representing himself
as a handsome and romantic young man
with a slightly mysterious glance
and with his arm nonchalantly resting on the base of a column.
The virtuoso treatment of the shades of precious silk
of his clothing highlight the fresh face and the golden hair
of the renowned artist,
the thirty-year-old "favourite of fortune".

169

The Room of Italian Majolica
By Leo von Klenze (1734–1864)
(Room 229)

This room, remarkable for its richly and varied
decor and semicircular riche completing it,
is used to display a magnificent collection
of sixteenth-century majolica. Italian decorative
sculpture adorns the centre of the hall; near
the walls are examples of furniture; pieces
of tapestry hang over them. Placed on special
stands are paintings, notably two masterpieces
by Raphael, a great master of the Renaissance.

170

Raphael (Raffaello Sanzio) (1483–1520)
The Conestabile Madonna. Ca 1503
Oil on canvas, transferred from a panel. 17.5 x 18 cm
Acquired 1870 from Count Conestabile
della Staffa in Perugia

This small-scale masterpiece created by the young Raphael
in his native Perugia, still bears some traces of the poetic style of
Perugino whose pupil the great master was. Raphael carefully and
lovingly portrayed the details of the face of the beautiful young
Madonna attentively looking into the book, the serious, concentrated
Child Christ, the details of the light spring landscape against the
background of which the figures are portrayed.
The picture was painted on a wooden panel and once it made up
a single whole with its frame said to have been produced from
Raphael's drawing. But the poor state of the wooden support made
Hermitage restorers, after the picture had arrived
from Italy in 1871, to transfer Raphael's priceless
painting onto canvas.

◀ 171
**The Study or the Room
of Frescoes
of the Raphael School
By Leo von Klenze
(1784–1864)**
(Room 230)

The nine frescoes devoted
to the life of Venus were
executed by Raphael's pupils
and came from the Palatine
villa which is believed
to have been the property
of Raphael himself.
In the nineteenth century
they were sold and
transferred onto canvas.
On accession to the
Hermitage in 1861 they
were already in a poor state,
but nevertheless, hung
on the walls of the room,
they perfectly add to the
Hermitage collection of High
Renaissance painting.
Displayed in this room
is now also *Crouching Boy*
by Michelangelo.

172
Michelangelo Buonarroti (1475–1564)
Crouching Boy. 1530s
Marble. Acquired 1785 from
the D. Lyde Browne collection

Almost all sculptural works by the great Italian
artist are in his homeland. This statue is
the Hermitage's only work by the titan
of the Renaissance. The surface of the piece
of marble used for the sculpture is not polished,
and the rough surface of the stone disperses
light. The face, hands and feet are barely
suggested which endows the image
with a special charm of vagueness and drama.
Such kind of treatment known as *non-finito*,
was characteristic of Michelangelo's
later period.
The small figure seems to be mighty
and creates an impression that is has
concentrated a huge yet
bound energy.

173, 174
The Knights' Hall
By Leo von Klenze (1784–1864)
(Room 243)

The hall designed by Klenze for a display of the Imperial
numismatic collection now houses the Hermitage's rich assemblage
of Western European arms and armour of the fifteenth
to seventeenth centuries.
The walls and ceiling of the Knights' Hall are adorned
with a rich ornamental painting and panels of artificial marble.
The inlaid parquet floor is made of valuable kinds of wood.
The variety of tournament and battle armour and cold arms –
from heavy two-handle swords to elegant stilettos, shields,
crossbows, helmets, pistols and muskets – are displayed
in the showcases alongside the walls.
In the centre of the huge hall one's attention is attracted
by a cavalcade of knights which vividly demonstrates various
items of arms and armour including protective coverings
for horses. The exhibition allows its visitors
to appreciate the virtuoso mastery and ingenuity of gunsmiths
and armourers in Italy, France, Germany
and England.

176 ▶
The Pavilion Hall
By Andrei Stakenschneider
(1802–1865)
(Room 204)

The architectural decoration
of the Pavilion Hall was
designed by Andrei
Stakenschneider and carried
out in 1850–58. In the same
period the architect created
the Winter Garden in which
luxuriant tropical plants grew
under a glass roof around
a fountain.
The four "fountains of tears",
based on motifs of the
Bakhchisarai Palace in the
Crimea, introduced elements
of Oriental architecture into
the luxurious interior
of the hall decorated with light
white arcades and magnificent
crystal chandeliers.
In 1939 the structures of the
Winter Garden were
dismantled.
Today the hall is used
for a display of the collection
of mosaic tables dating
from the nineteenth-century
and the famous Peacock
Clock.

◀ 175
The Pavilion Hall
Part of the interior
with a mantel clock
By Andrei Stakenschneider
(1802–1865)

This mantel clock is the work
of the French clockmaker Félix
Chopin active in St Petersburg
in the middle of the nineteenth
century. Its case of grey granite
is effectively combined with
the bronze figures of Cupid
and Psyche flanking the dial.
The focal point of the
composition is the ormolu
butterfly in Cupid's hand
which symbolizes Psyche's
tender and vibrant soul.
The figures are probably
by Pierre Philippe Thomire,
a leading French master
of bronzework in the early
nineteenth century. Formerly
the clock was in a living
apartment of the Winter Palace.

The Romanov Gallery
By Yury Velten (1730–1801)
(Rooms 259–262)

The galleries which connected the Northern
and Southern Pavilions of the Small Hermitage
were intended for imperial collections.
Velten completed their construction by 1775.
In the middle of the nineteenth century
the western gallery began to be called the
Romanov Gallery because it accommodated
a display of portraits of the ruling
Romanov dynasty.
At the present time it is used to display the
collection of Western European applied art most
of which entered the Hermitage in 1884,
when a huge and very valuable collection
of Anton Bazilewsky was purchased
in Paris.

---

178 ▼

The Virgin and Child. **Late 18th century**
France. Ebony. Acquired 1884 from
the A. P. Bazilewsky collection in Paris

In the thirteenth century Paris became the main
centre of ivory carving. The cult of the Madonna,
which became especially prominent in this
period, led to the production of numerous
statuettes. Subtly tinted, clad in long and wide
cloaks with freely descending folds, they stood
mainly in domestic chapels.

179

The Fortuny vase. 14th century. **Spain**
Acquired 1884 from the A. P. Bazilewsky
collection in Paris

A unique ceramic vase discovered near the Spanish
town of Malaga in 1871 by the eminent painter
Mariano Fortuny, is an outstanding example
of mediaeval applied art. The surface
of the vase is covered with a glistening, bluish glaze
called lustre, for which Malaga master craftsmen
were especially highly reputed.
The vase was intended for keeping water or wine
and usually was half-dug into the earth.

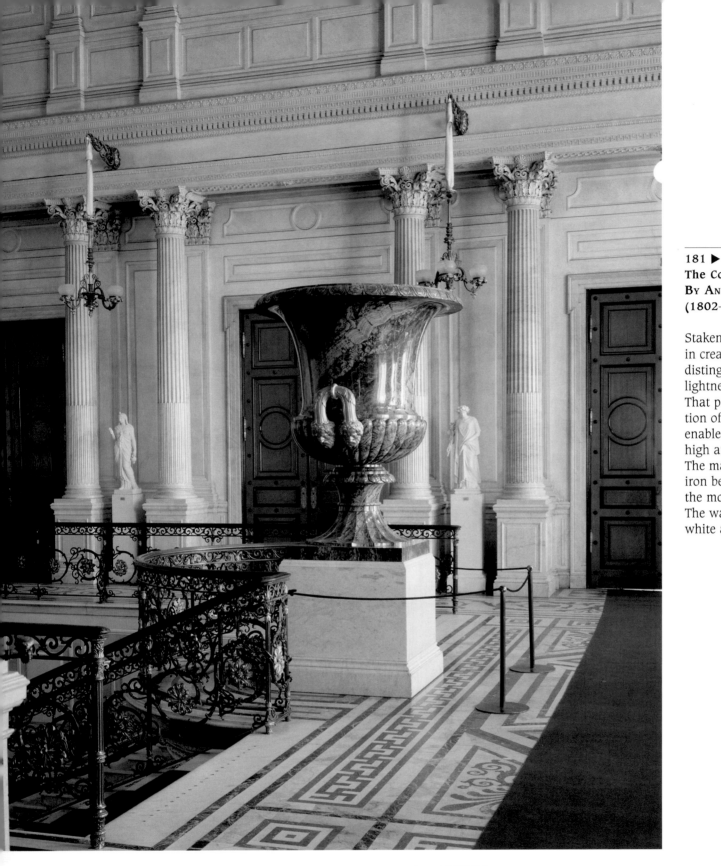

181 ▶

The Councillors' Staircase
By Andrei Stakenschneider
(1802–1865)

Stakenschneider succeeded
in creating an interior
distinguished both by
lightness and austere elegance.
That period saw an introduction of iron structures which
enabled the architect to use
high and steep flights.
The marble steps are set on
iron beams concealed under
the moulded decoration.
The walls are embellished with
white and crimson stuccowork.

180
The upper landing
of the Councillors' Staircase
By Andrei Stakenschneider (1802–1865)

The upper landing of the Councillors' Staircase is named
in honour of the State Council. In the middle of
the nineteenth century its sessions took place
in the halls of the ground floor of the Old Hermitage.
The landing occupies the place of the former Oval Room
created by Yury Velten in the 1780s.
The doors leading to the rooms of the Small,
Old and New Hermitages open
to the landing.

The Leonardo da Vinci Room
By Andrei Stakenschneder
(1802–1865)
(Room 214)

In the nineteenth century this room was known as the Italian Room, for its wall were decorated with works by Italian artists. Stakenschneider redesigned the entire suite of rooms of the Old Hermitage in 1858–60 to be used as living apartments which began to be named the Seventh Reserve Section. The room in which two masterpieces by Leonardo are displayed now, is notable for its luxurious decoration in imitation of French seventeenth-century Baroque forms. The doors of the room, adorned with an ornament of tortoise-shell and gilded metal, are executed in imitation of the Boulle technique. Over them are placed medallions with portraits of the Russian Field Marshals.

183

Leonardo da Vinci
(1452–1519)
*The Madonna and Child
(The Litta Madonna)
Ca 1490*

Tempera on canvas, transferred from a panel. 42 x 33 cm
Acquired 1865 from the Count Antonio Litta collection in Milan

In 1482 Leonardo was employed by Lodovico Moro, the Duke of Milan. At his court he painted, in the technique of tempera traditional for Italy, *The Madonna and Child* generally known as *The Litta Madonna* after her Italian owner, the Milanese Count Antonio Litta. The image of the Madonna embodies the High Renaissance ideal of beauty in which physical perfection is combined with spiritual elevation.

◀ 184
SIMONE MARTINI (CA 1284–1344)
The Madonna from *The Annunciation* scene
First half of the 14th century
Tempera on panel. 30.5 x 21.5 cm
Acquired 1911 as a bequest from the Count G. S. Stroganov
collection in Rome

Works by Simone Martini, the leading artist
of the Sienese school, can be extremely rarely
found in museum collections.
The Hermitage masterpiece is the right-hand
part of *The Annunciation* diptych.
The left wing with a representation of
the Archangel Gabriel is in the National Gallery
in Washington.
According to the mediaeval tradition,
Mary in the Annunciation scene is supposed
to be frightened and embarrassed,
but this state is rendered by Martini
with an exquisite, almost secular grace
and poetic subtlety.

185 ▶

FILIPPINO LIPPI (1457–1504)
The Adoration of the Infant Christ. Mid-1480s
Oil on copper, transferred from a panel, tondo,
dia. 53 cm. Acquired 1911 as a bequest
from the Count G. S. Stroganov
collection in Rome

The father of Filippino Lippi, Fra Filippo,
a well-known Florentine artist, was a monk in
his youth, but he ran away from the monastery
with a young nun who became his wife.
This romantic union brought forth the author
of *The Adoration of the Infant Christ*, whose
art is distinguished by noble elegance and
refinement. The poetic and sublime art of
Filippino Lippi was formed under the influence
of the great Quattrocento master Sandro
Botticelli. The artist depicted the Virgin and
the Child Christ amidst fragile, nearly fleshless
angels in Paradise, which is designated as
a small terrace separated by a balustrade from
a lifelike yet perfectly harmonious landscape.

186
PIETRO PERUGINO
(CA 1450–1523)
St Sebastian. Ca 1495
Tempera and oil on panel
53.5 x 39.5 cm
Acquired 1910 from
the Marquise N. V. Catanari
collection in Rome

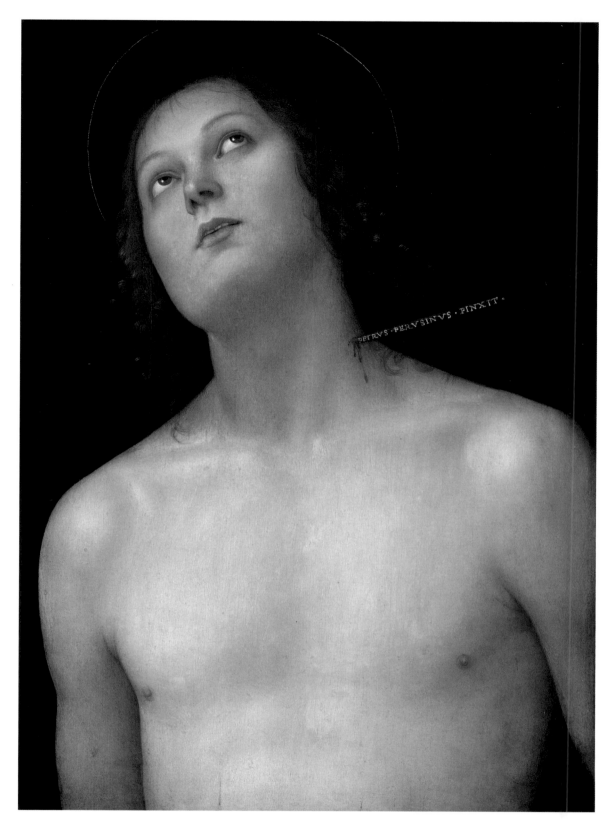

Pietro Perugino is a major master of the Early Renaissance,
a representative of the Umbrian school of painting,
Raphael's teacher.
The tragic and beautiful image of the saint painted by Perugino
is imbued with an almost elegiac sorrow, calm and neglect
of earthly things.
On the arrow which pierced the saint's neck,
the artist put his signature in gold: *Petrus Perusinus pinxit*
("Painted by Pietro Perugino").

The HERMITAGE

A State Museum: The 20th Century

THE HERMITAGE
IN THE REIGN OF THE LAST ROMANOV

*Portrait of Empress
Alexandra Fiodorovna*
By Mikhail Rundaltsov. 1905
Oil on canvas

◀◀ **"Beneath the Sign of
the Eagle". The new exhibition
in the General Staff building.
The former Drawing-Room
in the apartments of Karl
Nesselrode, the Chancellor
of the Russian Empire**
By Carlo Rossi. 1820–27

◀ *Portrait of
Emperor Nicholas II*
By Nikolai Kuznetsov
1915–16
Oil on canvas

On 24 October 1894 Emperor Alexander III died in the palace of Livadia in the Crimea. He was succeeded by Nicholas II, under whom Russia entered the twentieth century. Society was astir with presentiments of imminent change, vague hopes and alarms. There were few, however, who in 1894 believed that this young man would be the last occupant of the Russian throne. More than twenty years remained before the revolution and the fall of the monarchy. Nicholas himself, in the autumn he took charge of his immense realm, lived a life that swung between sorrow and joy: on 7 November his father was interred in the SS Peter and Paul Cathedral; a week later, on 14 November, Nicholas was celebrating his marriage to the woman he had long been determined to marry, Princess Alix of Hesse-Darmstadt. He waited for his fiancée, who had taken the name Alexandra Fiodorovna on conversion to Orthodoxy, to emerge from the Malachite Room in the Winter Palace, where the age-old ritual of dressing the bride took place. The modest wedding ceremony was also held in the palace, in the Great Church.

With the new, young imperial couple life returned to the Winter Palace. Alexander III had disliked the place, preferring other residences, and in his reign the Winter Palace had been reserved for official ceremonies. Nicholas and Alexandra made the old dwelling place of Russian emperors their home. The second-storey living apartments overlooking the Neva and Admiralty were redecorated to designs by Alexander Krasovsky (1848–1923). The architect also supervised the work that took a year and on 30 December 1895 the imperial couple, with their newly-born daughter Grand Duchess Olga, moved into the palace. Nicholas II's simple, austerely decorated rooms faced the Admiralty. Those visiting the palace on official business entered the sovereign's apartments by the western, Saltykov, entrance. After waiting in the adjutant's room for an invitation from the duty valet, they walked through the Billiard Room and Library to the Tsar's study. Nicholas spent long hours working there every day, receiving reports, listening to court and government officials and signing documents. The Tsar had no personal secretary. Fearful of entrusting his thoughts and opinions to someone else, he preferred to write letters and documents himself, and even to apply the stamp with his own hand. Only important official papers were prepared for the sovereign's signature in the imperial chancelleries. When his work in the study was done, Nicholas hurried to rejoin his family.

In earlier times the Russian rulers' private and public existences seemed inextricably combined. Tradition demanded that the Emperor and Empress live to a large extent separate lives, each in their own apartments, the monarch dealing with affairs of state, his spouse with the family and charitable concerns. However, a trend towards a more "democratic" life-style had spread to the Russian aristocracy and to the imperial family. Nicholas and Alexandra lived like an ordinary couple, sharing their interests and concerns with one another. Moreover, contemporaries are unanimous in noting the deep mutual attachment between the royal pair. This all left its mark on the way of life in the Winter Palace under Nicholas II.

Nicholas's apartments led directly into the private rooms of Alexandra Fiodorovna. The Tsar's study lay next to the Empress's boudoir and bedroom. This last room was cosily fitted out with comfortable modern furniture, a display chest containing a large number of icons, and photographs of relatives on the walls. Beyond the bedroom were the drawing-rooms, the most luxurious of which was the Malachite Room which Alexandra left as it had been under its previous owner, the wife of Nicholas I. The last Russian Empress felt strong ties with those royal spouses who had lived in the same rooms before her. It is no coincidence that she always had hanging above her desk a portrait of Empress Elizabeth Alexeyevna, the wife of Alexander I and the first occupant of these apartments in the Winter Palace.

The Malachite Room served as a state room: on major occasions the courtiers waited here for the imperial family to leave their private apartments and begin their formal procession. The Emperor led the way with Dowager Empress Maria Fiodorovna, followed by Empress Alexandra accompanied by one of the Grand Dukes, then came members of the family, the court, the diplomatic corps and guests who gradually joined the ranks of those passing through the suite of state rooms to the Great Church. From there, after the service, they all proceeded to the St George Hall where the official part of the ceremony was held.

One of the most impressive and attractive ceremonies in Nicholas's time was the Blessing of the Waters at Epiphany. Each year, for 6 January, a carpeted dais was constructed on the bank of the Neva by the palace and, below it, a round wooden pavilion with a pale blue dome scattered with gold stars was raised directly on the frozen surface of the river. Beneath this rotunda, a cross-shaped hole was cut in the ice. It was called a Jordan in commemoration of the river in which Christ was baptized. On the morning of Epiphany, after the Tsar's inspection of troops in the palace state rooms and a service in the Great Church, the ceremony proper began. As the weather was usually cold the two Empresses, past and present, the Grand Duchesses and their attendants remained in the palace and watched the ceremony through the Empress's windows. The Emperor, accompanied by other members of the imperial house, senior officers and clergy descended the main staircase of the palace and went out to the Neva. (Both the staircase and the adjoining entrance acquired the name "Jordan".) The metropolitan held a service in the rotunda and sprinkled newly-blessed, ice-cold Neva water on the regimental standards and all those present to the accompaniment of a cannon salute. Then the whole grand procession returned to the warmth of palace by the Jordan Staircase.

The Wedding of Emperor Nicholas II and Empress Alexandra Fiodorovna
By Loritz Tuxen. 1895
Oil on canvas

The favourite events for the imperial family, the court and the whole of St Petersburg high society in those early years were the balls held in the Winter Palace. The season of court balls opened every year with the Grand Ball in the St Nicholas Hall, to which some 1,000 guests were invited — courtiers, foreign diplomats and officers of the elite regiments. Balls were held not only in the state rooms of the palace, but also in the Pavilion Hall of the Small Hermitage. Quite often they were accompanied by performances in the Hermitage Theatre and ended with supper in the halls of the palace, sometimes in the New Hermitage as well.

On ordinary days the heavy gilded doors of the Malachite Room were kept shut. Beyond them, in the apartments of the Emperor and Empress, the family lived its normal life. Several times a day they gathered in the Small Dining-Room. (That room, exquisitely decorated in the French Rococo style still retains the appearance it had under the last Romanovs.) The adults — the august parents and a few particularly close invited guests — were always joined by the children. The first daughter, Olga, was followed by three others: Tatiana, Maria and Anastasia. The rooms created for the Grand Duchesses on the ground floor of the Winter Palace had their own entrance on the Neva side of the building (it has not survived), but were linked directly to the Empress's apartments. Alexandra devoted much time to her children, concerning herself with every aspect of their upbringing. She made music, did needlework and painting with the Grand Duchesses. She had long talks with them, instilling her own deeply-felt moral and religious convictions, as well as — particularly unusual in aristocratic families at that time — a love of work, ordinary, everyday toil. Parents and children in the family of the last Russian tsar enjoyed a relationship of friendship and trust. In winter Nicholas was fond of skating with his daughters on the rink in the Great Courtyard of the Winter Palace; in spring in the same place he tended the flowers and trees in the garden with them. This was very different from the traditional behaviour of Russian rulers and their families. The same warm ties existed between the royal parents. Contemporaries recalled how in the evenings Nicholas and his wife would withdraw to the Tsar's library, where in the quiet after the concerns of the day they talked for a long time, read and looked through books and albums. Sometimes when they came back late from the theatre, they made themselves a small supper for two in the library.

The idyllic family life of the last Russian Tsar was, however, constantly clouded by alarms and anxieties. Nicholas's reign was marked by an ever-growing revolutionary movement. The tense situation

Part of the Study of Empress
Alexandra Fiodorovna
in the Winter Palace
(reconstruction). Bureau,
1890s–1900s;
chair, 1890s, St Petersburg
*Portrait of Empress
Elizabeth Alexeyevna*
By Louise Elisabeth
Vigée-Lebrun. 18th century

The Study of Emperor
Nicholas II
in the Winter Palace
Early 20th century. Photograph

inside the country was made worse by failures in the sphere of foreign policy. The war with Japan that broke out in January 1904 ended in August 1905 with a serious defeat. It provoked a profound social and political crisis in Russia. The resultant revolution was only put down at great cost by the end of 1907. With harsh repressive measures, using the army, the police and the courts, the Tsar strove to save the absolute monarchy in which he earnestly believed.

The situation was made worse by the fact that for many years the monarch had no male heir. The long-awaited son was born on 30 July 1904 at Peterhof, the summer residence of the imperial family. At his baptism, he was given a name that had belonged to two notable members of the Romanov dynasty – Peter the Great's father Alexis (Alexei) Mikhailovich, and his son Tsarevich Alexis (whom Peter had executed). The joyful appearance of an heir soon turned, however, into a profound drama: Alexis was found to be suffering from a serious inherited disorder – haemophilia – that prevented his blood from clotting, turning the smallest cut or bruise into a very grave, even life-threatening matter. The Tsesarevich's illness obliged the imperial family to give up life in St Petersburg and the Winter Palace. The Alexander Palace in the suburb of Tsarskoye Selo to the south of the capital was chosen as the new winter residence for the Emperor and his family.

It was there that the worst years of the last Tsar's reign were spent. The family lived in constant anxiety about the heir to the throne and the future of the dynasty that he embodied. The Empress, despairing of help from doctors, prayed fervently for a miracle. Her deep religious faith grew obsessive and a succession of faith healers, quacks and mystics appeared at court. The last was the sinister figure of the "holy-man" Grigory Rasputin. That semiliterate Siberian peasant, who undoubtedly had a hypnotic gift, was able in some mysterious way to relieve Alexis's sufferings and arrest the bleeding during his haemophilic attacks. Rasputin's influence over the Empress was immense and many sought to exploit him to obtain what they wanted from the Tsar. Indignation in Russian society reached bursting point and in December 1916, Rasputin was killed in the home of Felix Yusupov, a young nobleman who had become a close relative of the Tsar by marriage.

Meanwhile the Winter Palace stood empty. Silence reigned in the splendid state rooms and the cosy private apartments, where only the servants remained to keep things in order. In the eyes of Russia and Europe, however, the palace remained a magnificent symbol of autocratic power and the might of the empire. The main official ceremonies, important acts of state and celebrations still took place there. On 19 February 1913 the Tsar and his family returned to the Winter Palace for the festivities marking three hundred years of the Romanov dynasty. The 21 February was the exact anniversary of Mikhail Fiodorovich, the first member of the dynasty, being summoned to the throne by an assembly representing the whole Russian nation. The celebrations lasted several days: formal processions alternated with receptions of deputations from all corners of Russia; gala dinners in the state rooms for representatives of the nobility, municipalities, peasantry and diplomatic corps with suppers shared with courtiers in the family's private apartments.

The last Romanov still had four years left to rule. The year after the celebrations, the First World War broke out. On 20 July 1914, the day after Germany declared war on Russia, the imperial family drove into St Petersburg, to the Winter Palace, leaving the sickly Alexis in Peterhof. Here the Tsar signed the Manifesto on War with Germany. Nicholas II processed with his family and court from the Malachite Hall to the St Nicholas Hall where the manifesto was proclaimed and a service was held.

Thus began the most tragic days in the history of the Russian monarchy and the main imperial residence. On 6 January 1914 the last grand ceremony of the Blessing of the Waters had taken place. For the palace, life in wartime was harder than it had ever been. In 1915 a military hospital (named after the heir to the throne) was installed in the building. The Jordan Staircase became the reception area from which the wounded were taken to wards located in the state rooms of the palace. The hospital was under the personal patronage of the Empress and her elder daughters, Olga and Tatiana. They all three worked here as nurses, participating in operations and tending the wounded. Beyond the palace walls, however, in the capital and throughout Russia, a mighty wave of general dissatisfaction was growing. The war undermined once and for all the foundations of the old order. The autocratic monarchy proved incapable of dealing with the army's heavy casualties and defeats, the country's poverty and devastation, the people's misery and degradation. Spontaneous disaffection rapidly assumed the form of an organized revolutionary movement. The political parties that had appeared at the beginning of the century demanded civil rights, a constitution, and the most radical of them – above all the Bolshevik wing of the Social Democrats – called for an end to the monarchy. Russia was on the brink of revolution. The Winter Palace was about to lose its status as a royal residence.

The fate of the Imperial Hermitage was always inseparably linked to that of the residence. However, although it was the property of the ruling family, the Hermitage under the last Romanovs functioned effectively as a separate institution. The position of the museum from the late nineteenth century onward was not easy. Neither Alexander III nor Nicholas II displayed any great interest in the Hermitage. The tsars and members of their family rarely appeared in the museum, mainly during festivities, balls and gala dinners that, despite the obvious inappropriateness and direct threat to the works of art, were from time to time organized in its halls. The Ministry of the Court to which the Hermitage was subordinated drew its own conclusions from this and restricted the museum's funding.

At the same time there was a tremendous growth of interest in the Hermitage among the Russian intelligentsia. The possibility of admiring some of the greatest achievements of culture in one of the world's greatest museums, as the Hermitage by then was, drew not only curious foreign travellers and citizens of the capital, but also people who came from the Russian provinces. The number of visitors to the Hermitage grew with every year. In 1903 alone, over 130,000 people passed through its halls. All restrictions on entry to the museum had been lifted. School pupils with their tutors became an increasingly common sight and shortly before the revolution groups from the workers' Sunday schools even began to appear, brought by their teachers. Such educators were the first to give guided tours of the museum. All guidebooks to St Petersburg included plans of the Hermitage displays and descriptions of the main collections and most important exhibits.

The public interest was a source of no small support for the Hermitage curators. At this time the most outstanding historians and art experts were working in the museum. They were engaged in compiling catalogues and writing detailed guides to the museum. The scientific study of the Hermitage's stocks represented a considerable contribution to Russian and world art-history. The curators made every effort to maintain and expand the museum, despite financial difficulties and severe budgetary restrictions. New acquisitions were relatively rare under the last Romanovs and no longer systematic as before. Sometimes pieces were simply transferred to the Hermitage from a room in the Winter Palace or one of the other residences. Jean Honoré Fragonard's *Snatched Kiss*, now one of the most notable paintings in the display of French art, was acquired from the Lazienkowski Palace in Warsaw in exchange for the Hermitage's *Polish Girl* by Antoine Watteau. The Hermitage also grew during this period thanks to the love and generosity of private collectors. Over fifty years the noted Russian geographer, traveller and researcher into Central Asia and the Orient, Piotr Semionov-Tian-Shansky used his own very modest means to put together a collection of Small Dutch Masters. From the outset he intended the collection to go to the Hermitage and was guided by the museum's existing stocks of seventeenth-century Dutch painting, striving to buy those artists who were not already represented. His collection of over 700 works, well known to all lovers and scholars of Dutch art, was presented to the Hermitage in 1910, but finally moved to the museum only after the collector's death four years later. Thanks to this act, the Hermitage came to own one of the world's finest collections of paintings by the Small Dutch Masters, now numbering over 1,000 works. In 1911 and 1912 the Hermitage became the richer by several masterpieces of early Italian painting bequeathed by the well-known aristocrats Grigory and Pavel Stroganov. A highly valuable addition to the museum in that same period was an outstanding work by the great Spanish painter El Greco, *The Apostles Peter and Paul* presented by its owner General Durnovo. This painting, believed to be by an unknown master, was shown at an exhibition of private collections organized in St Petersburg in 1908 by the noted art periodical *Stariye Gody*. The authorship of El Greco was established by the chief curator of the Picture Gallery, Ernest Liphart (1847–1932). Liphart, a well-known portrait-painter (pupil of his own father who was a brilliant connoisseur of art), lived in Italy for over ten years and was very familiar with all the museums and art treasures of that country. A painter's talent, an artist's keen eye, tremendous erudition, taste and intuition made Liphart a shrewd, astute, devoted guardian of the Hermitage's paintings. It is to Liphart that the museum owes the greatest acquisition made in the last years of its imperial history. That was Leonardo da Vinci's *Madonna with a Flower*, known as *The Benois Madonna*. The painting, again held to be the work of an unknown master, belonged to the family of the noted St Petersburg architect Leonty Benois. When he saw it at the exhibition of private collections in 1908, Liphart persuasively argued that it was an early work by Leonardo. His attribution was supported by all major art scholars. Still, the curator had to exert great efforts to persuade the Ministry of the Court and a specially formed commission from the Academy of Arts that the masterpiece must be bought. In 1914 the *Benois Madonna* adorned the Hermitage's Italian collection. This acquisition ended the history of the Hermitage under the Romanovs. War was raging, revolution just around the corner. The Hermitage stood on the threshold of a new chapter in its existence.

189 ▶
The Small Dining-Room
BY ALEXANDER KRASOVSKY (1848–1923)
(Room 188)

The Small Dining-Room served as a place
of family meals and at the same time
it linked the living apartments of the royal family
with the other rooms of the Winter Palace.
The three windows of the Dining-Room overlook
the inner courtyard and therefore artificial light
was mainly used for its illumination.
The architect stylized the space in an imitation
of the Rococo style.
The walls of the Small, or White Dining-Room,
as it was sometimes named, are decorated
with mid-eighteenth-century tapestries woven by
masters of the St Petersburg Tapestry Factory.
Three of them are allegories of the parts of the world,
Asia, *Africa* and *America*, and the fourth
one is known as *Swans*.
The furnishings of the room have been completely
preserved because it has a memorial meaning –
it was in this room
that during the night of 25 to 26 October
(from 7 to 8 November New Style)
the Provisional Government was arrested.

187, 188
The Library of Nicholas II
BY ALEXANDER KRASOVSKY (1848–1923)
(Room 178)

The decoration of the living apartments of
Nicholas II began in the middle of the 1890s.
Only two interiors, the Library and the Small
Dining-Room have survived in a good state.
The Library is one of the best examples of room
intended for this purpose. Nearly square in its
configuration, it was well lit through three
windows overlooking the Admiralty. Seventeen
bookcases arranged in line along the walls were
executed at a high artistic level with a wide use
of motifs of carved Gothic ornaments –
lanceolate arches, pierced trefoils, four-leaved
rosettes. The same kind of bookcases was used
on the choir which can be reached by a narrow
two-flight wooden staircase. The Library was
provided with three large tables and two
armchairs of the "comfortable" type.

191 ▶
LEONARDO DA VINCI
(1452–1519)
*The Madonna with a Flower
(The Benois Madonna).* 1478
Oil on canvas, transferred from
a panel. 49.5 x 31.5 cm
Acquired 1914 from the M. A. Benois
collection in St Petersburg

The history of how this masterpiece by Leonardo came to St Petersburg is very interesting. The picture was the property of the Astrakhan merchant Sapozhnikov, whose daughter married the St Petersburg architect Leonty Benois. Sapozhnikov told that he had acquired this painting at Astrakhan from a strolling Italian musician. Later this beautiful legend was refuted, but it still remains a mystery when and how this unique work from the great artist's early period arrived in Russia. The work is painted in the technique of oil painting which was new in that period.

190
EL GRECO (DOMENIKOS THEOTOKOPOULOS) (1541–1614)
The Apostles Peter and Paul. Between 1587 and 1582
Oil on canvas. 121.5 x 105 cm
Acquired 1911 as a gift of P. P. Durnovo
in St Petersburg

In the twentieth century the collection of the Hermitage, basically formed within the preceding century, continued to be enriched with masterpieces of European painting. General Durnovo presented to the museum a magnificent work by the great Spanish artist El Greco. The painting is evidently based on the Gospel scene illustrating the only conflict between the two Apostles when the resolute and undaunted St Paul rebuked the meek St Peter for his inconsistency revealed during their conversion of pagans to Christianity at Antioch.

196 ▶

THOMAS GAINSBOROUGH
(1727–1788)
Portrait of a Lady in Blue
Late 1770s
Oil on canvas. 76 x 64 cm
Acquired 1912–16 as a bequest
of A. Z. Khitrovo in Petrograd

On entering the Hermitage
collection this masterpiece
by Gainsborough was listed
as a portrait of the Duchess
de Beaufort, the wife
of the French ambassador
to the English court. However,
there is no evidence that
Gainsborough painted anybody
from the duke's family.
Lofty and splendid to this day
as a romantic dream,
the stranger still remains
a mysterious "lady in blue".

195

THOMAS LAWRENCE (1769–1830)
Portrait of Count Mikhail Vorontsov. 1821
Oil on canvas. 143 x 113 cm
Acquired 1923 from the State Museum Fund,
earlier in the Vorontsov-Dashkov family collection in Petrograd

Count Vorontsov took part in the Patriotic War of 1812
and was wounded in the Battle of Borodino.
In 1819, on coming to London
for a visit to his father, the Russian ambassador in England,
together with his young wife, he commissioned his formal portrait
to Thomas Lawrence, the most fashionable English painter of this period.
The portrait of the count, who is represented
in the uniform of a general, with the three stars of the Russian orders,
features the romantic image of victor and hero.

◀ **197**
The enfilade of rooms
of 18th-century French art
in the Winter Palace
(Rooms 283–289)

In the 1920s the former living
apartments of the Winter
Palace were transformed into
museum displays. Today these
rooms designed after the fire
of 1837 by the architect
Alexander Briullov house
the collection of French art
of the seventeenth and
eighteenth centuries,
the largest outside France.

198
CORNEILLE DE LYONS (EARLY 16TH CENTURY – CA 1575)
Female Portrait. 1530s–1540s
Oil on panel. 20 x 15.5 cm
Acquired 1925 from the Shuvalov
family collection in Petrograd

Works by famous Renaissance French artists can be rarely found beyond
the boundaries of France. One of them, Corneille de Lyons, a Fleming
by birth, came to France in the reign of Francis I.
Although the artist spent his entire life at Lyons. he became court painter
to the Kings Charles IX and Henri II. The Hermitage portrait
by the artist is an excellent example
of his virtuoso skill.

◀ 199
**FRANÇOIS BOUCHER
(1703–1770)**
*Landscape in the Environs
of Beauvais*. Early 1740s
Oil on canvas. 49 x 58 cm
Acquired 1925 through the State
Museum Fund from
the E. P. and M. S. Oliv collection

There was a tapestry factory
at Beauvais near Paris where
Boucher worked since 1734.
His *Landscape in the Environs
of Beauvais* is a vivid
decorative painting well fitting
a Rococo-style interior.

200 ▶
JEAN MARC NATTIER (1685–1766)
Portrait of a Lady in Grey. 1750s (?)
Oil on canvas. 80 x 64 cm (oval). Acquired 1920 through
the State Museum Fund from the P. P. Durnovo collection
in Petrograd

Nattier was an excellent painter and a
fashionable portraitist of the Rococo period.
His works are not marked by the depth
of penetration into the character portrayed –
on the contrary, the artist so skilfully flattered
his models that all his customers, especially
women, while retaining their individual
features, looked young and beautiful
in his portraits.

201
WILLEM CLAESZ HEDA (1594 – BETWEEN 1680 AND 1682)
Breakfast with a Crab. 1648
Oil on canvas. 118 x 118 cm
Acquired 1920 from the State Museum Fund

This still life belongs to the "monochrome breakfasts" type of Heda's paintings.
The colour scheme of his painting is nearly devoid of bright shades yet the combination of greyish-
olive, golden and white tones creates a noble and subtle colour scheme. The seemingly casual
disposition of things in the composition with its overturned goblet, crumpled table-cloth
and plate shifted to the edge of the table — conceals, however,
the artist's subtle calculation and inner balance.

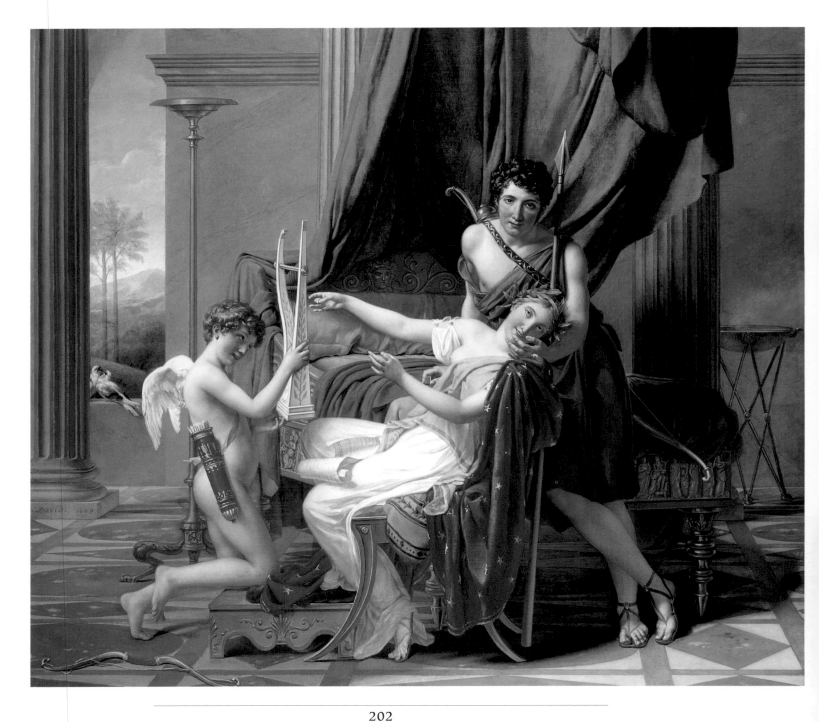

202

Jacques-Louis David (1748–1825)
Sappho and Phaon. 1809
Oil on canvas. 225 x 262 cm. Commissioned by Prince N. B. Yusupov
Transferred 1925 from the Yusupov Palace in Leningrad

This panting was commissioned from the celebrated creator of Neo-Classicism
by Prince Nikolai Yusupov. The image of Sappho, a famous ancient Greek
poetess, attracted many Neo-Classical artists. Already not young, she fell in love
with the young Phaon and took a suicide unable to suffer the pains of
unrequited love. Everything in this picture is sustained in the spirit of classical
examples – from the subject and the heroes' clothes to the details
of furniture and garments which David modelled,
after a thorough study, on works of ancient art.

203 ▶

FRANÇOIS GÉRARD (1770–1837)
Portrait of Joséphine de Beauharnais. 1801
Oil on canvas. 178 x 174 cm
Acquired 1919 from the Duke of Leuchtenberg
collection in Petrograd

Joséphine (1763–1814) was married to General
Alexandre de Beauharnais and later became
the first wife of Napoleon Bonaparte their
marriage lasting from 1796 to 1809.
The Empress of France between 1804 and 1809.
The well-known portrait painter Gérard,
a pupil of David, painted Joséphine
on the terrace of her Malmaison Palace near
Paris. This was then a novel, Neo-Classical
type of formal portraiture, intently devoid
of luxury and abundant accessories typical
of commissioned portraits popular
in the previous period.

204
ANTOINE-JEAN GROS (1771–1835)
Napoleon Bonaparte at the Arcole Bridge
**The artist's replica of the painting
produced in 1797**
Oil on canvas. 134 x 101 cm. Acquired 1924 through
the State Museum Fund from the Duke of Leuchtenberg
collection in Leningrad

Gros, the favourite pupil of Jacques Louis David,
the head of the Neo-Classical school, depicts General
Napoleon Bonaparte (1769–1821) during a moment
of his triumph. The young commander of the French
army is shown during a battle against the Austrian
troops at Arcole in Italy (15–17 November 1796).
Gros, like many of his contemporaries, admired the
personality of the future Emperor of France and
accompanied Napoleon in his Italian campaign.
During the battle at the Arcole bridge,
when the victory of the Austrians seemed to be
imminent, Napoleon rushed forward with a banner
in his hands, inspiring his soldiers
and won the battle.

◀ 205

CONSTANTINE TROYON
(1810–1865)
On the Way to the Market
1859
Oil on canvas. 260.5 x 211 cm
Acquired 1922 through the Museum
of the Academy of Arts;
formerly the Kushelev Gallery
in Petrograd

Troyon, a well-known Salon
painter, took an interest in the
work of the Barbizon artists
and frequently joined them
on painting tours in the
picturesque environs of their
favourite Forest of
Fontainebleau. His large-scale
paintings featuring herds of
cows and sheep wandering
along roads or grazing around
Barbizon enjoyed such
a great success with art lovers
that he could hardly cope
with a wave of commissions.

206
EUGÈNE DELACROIX (1798–1863)
Arab Saddling His Horse. 1855
Oil on canvas. 56 x 47 cm
Acquired 1922 from the Museum of the Academy of Arts;
formerly the Kushelev Gallery in Petrograd

The great Delacroix treated Oriental motifs with all the passion
of his unbridled Romantic temperament.
The artist travelled to Algeria and Morocco as early as 1832,
but twenty years later Moroccan impressions sounded as
a spontaneous and powerful chord in his paintings.
A seemingly ordinary occurrence captured by the artist's swift
brush, is pervaded with energy and dynamism. In a few minutes
the fleeting scene. which evokes a sense of inner unity
of the man and his horse, will disappear.

◀ 207
JEAN-LOUIS GÉRÔME (1824–1904)
The Sale of a Slave. 1884
Oil on canvas. 92 x 74 cm
Acquired 1930 through the Antiquariat;
formerly the collection
of Grand Duchess
Yelizaveta Fiodorovna
in St Petersburg

The most notable figure among Salon painters,
Gérôme was granted nearly all kinds
of official honours, titles and awards which
a French artist could dream of –
medals of the Salon, the Légion d'Honneur,
the title of Academician, etc..
The Sale of a Slave had a tremendous
success in the Salon of 1884 where
it was displayed as *The Sale of Slaves
in Rome.*

208 ▶
LOUIS LEOPOLD BOILLY
(1761–1845)
Billiards. 1807
Oil on canvas. 56 x 81 cm
Acquired 1925 from the Yusupov
Palace Museum in Leningrad

This painting was bought
by Nikolai Yusupov in Paris.
The best of the nine Hermitage
canvases by Boilly, a well-
known genre painter, it shows
elegant women in tight-fitting
dresses who are playing the
game of billiards. This subject,
impossible during the earlier
period, indicates the radical
changes which took place
in society after the revolution.
In the early nineteenth
century, a billiards room
became a sort of club where
people gathered not only
to play but to exchange news,
to make acquaintances
and to flirt.

209
EMILE AUGUSTE-CHARLES CAROLUS-DURANT
(1838–1917)
Portrait of Nadezhda Polovtsova. 1876
Oil on canvas. 206.5 x 124.5 cm
Received 1926 from the A. L. Stieglitz Museum; formerly the A. A. Polovtscv collection in Leningrad

This portrait of Nadezhda Mikhailovna Polovtsova, adopted daughter of Baron Alexander Stieglitz, wife of Alexander Polovtsov, a member of the State Council, was painted by the fashionable Salon painter of the second half of the nineteenth century in Paris. Carolus-Durant was famous for his amazingly quick yet virtuoso rendering of the sleekly beautiful faces and hands of aristocratic female customers, the resplendence of their rich garments and the shimmer of gemstones.

210

CLAUDE MONET (1840–1926)
The Pond at Montgeron. 1876
Oil on canvas. 173 x 193 cm
Acquired 1931 from the Museum
of New Western Art in Moscow;
formerly the I. A. Morozov collection
in Moscow

Monet completely abandoned the traditional approach to painting
and composition evolved in the seventeenth century and
exemplified by Lorrain's classical landscapes. Even his monumental *Pond at Montgeron*, produced for the decoration of the villa
of the art collector Hochédé, a financier and an admirer of
Impressionism, which was a rare thing in that period, was an
immediate study painted out of doors. The picture has no clear-cut
planes, the objects on the canvas cannot be divided into main
and auxiliary ones, and the wide, divided brushstrokes look like
a chaotic mass of pigments at a closer examination.
But at some distance there arises a striking feeling of a real
scene vibrant in sunlight.

211
CLAUDE MONET (1840–1926)
A Poppy Field. Late 1880s
Oil on canvas. 59 x 90 cm. Acquired 1948 from the Museum
of New Western Art in Moscow;
before 1925, in the Tretyakov Gallery, Moscow;
formerly the I. A. Morozov collection in Moscow

To work directly from nature capturing the immediate visual
impression in all the variety of colour hues at a particular moment
and in particular conditions of light — that was the main task
faced by Monet and his friends. Such artistic method naturally led
Monet to painting the same motifs several times.
As a result, his paintings varying in their colour schemes but
similar in subject matter and bearing the same name. *Poppy Field,*
can be met in different museums of the world.

212
Pierre Auguste Renoir
(1841–1919)
Portrait of Jeanne Samary
1878
Oil on canvas. 173 x 103 cm
Acquired 1948 from the Museum
of New Western Art in Moscow;
formerly the M. A. Morozov
collection in Moscow

The charming red-haired
woman standing still in front
of Renoir for a classical formal
portrait is Jeanne Samary,
an actress of the Comédie-
Française. It seems that she
would soon drop her hands,
give us her enchanting smile
and swiftly disappear leaving
behind only a memory of her
beautiful blue eyes, white skin
and silk dress notable for
a wealth of its shades.
It is difficult to imagine that
this beautiful woman
portrayed by the delighted
Renoir in the prime of her life,
would pass away at the age
of thirty-three.

213 ▶
Pierre Auguste Renoir
(1841–1919)
Child with a Whip. 1885
Oil on canvas. 105 x 75 cm
Acquired 1948 from the Museum
of New Western Art in Moscow;
formerly the I. A. Morozov collection
in Moscow

The main hero in this painting is sunlight. It seems to dissolve the boy's figure
in the natural environment tinting his white dress and the sandy path with greenish,
yellow and bluish hues. However, the oval of the childish face, the dark large eyes
and the bright pouting lips of the small boy, whose name was Etienne Goujon,
are painted out in a careful and clear-cut manner, apparently different
from the Impressionist principles. In the period when this picture was produced,
Renoir was searching for a novel artistic manner that would combine the spontaneity
of Impressionism with the classical deliberation prevalent
in the preceding eighteenth century.

214
Paul Cézanne (1839–1906)
Still Life with Curtain. Ca 1899
Oil on canvas. 53 x 72 cm. Acquired 1930 from the Museum
of New Western Art in Moscow; formerly the I. A. Morozov
collection in Moscow

Cézanne arrived at Paris from his native Aix-en-
Provence in the 1860s as a mature and original
master. The Impressionists helped him avoid
a dark colour scheme, yet his paintings would
never adhere to their pictorial system. In his still
lifes Cézanne, similarly to the Impressionists,
does not dissolve his details in the air medium,
yet he neither seeks to render the texture of
the objects. The artist models the volumes of the
fruit, vessels and the folds of the curtain not
by means of light and shade as Old Masters did,
but by alternating warm and cold hues. Solving
this difficult task, he deliberately arranged
his still lifes from simple objects which would
resemble a ball, a cylinder or a cone.

215
Paul Cézanne (1839–1906)
Smoker. Ca 1895
Oil on canvas. 91 x 72 cm
Acquired 1931 from the Museum
of New Western Art in Moscow;
formerly the I. A. Morozov
collection in Moscow

Portraying people, Cézanne did not seek to convey
the psychological states or characters of his sitters.
Man is for him primarily the most complex
and interesting form created by nature.
The artist had his models pose for him for a long time,
in some cases up to a hundred sittings,
trying to understand the austere logic and balance
of their structures.

216
VINCENT VAN GOGH (1853–1890)
The Ladies of Arles. 1888
Oil on canvas. 73.5 x 92.5 cm
Acquired 1948 from the Museum
of New Western Art in Moscow;
formerly the S. I. Shchukin collection
in Moscow

This picture has another title,
The Memory of the Garden at Etten.
The artist combines here his impressions of the Arles period and
his recollection of his father's house
in Holland where his childhood
and youth had passed.

◀ 217

VINCENT VAN GOGH (1853–1890)
Cottages. 1890
Oil on canvas. 60 x 73 cm
Acquired 1948 from the Museum
of New Western Art in Moscow;
formerly the I. A. Morozov collection
in Moscow

This canvas was painted at Auvers, several
months before the artist's tragic death.
Van Gogh had no hope to cure from his mental
illness any more. But the painting has no tragic
overtones. The motif is treated in a light
gamut and only sharp open brushstrokes evidence
to the artist's state.

218

VINCENT VAN GOGH (1853–1890)
The Lilac Bush. 1889
Oil on canvas. 72 x 92 cm
Acquired 1948 from the Museum of New Western Art
in Moscow; formerly the S. I. Shchukin
collection in Moscow

This picture was painted by Van Gogh in May 1889, in the garden
of the San-Rémy Hospital where he took cure after one of his usual
attacks of mental illness. During a period of temporary abatement
of suffering, he created this masterpiece endowing the study
with an unusual dramatic feeling and profound symbolic message.
In the blossoming lilac bush thrusting its branches
to the heavens, but firmly rooted in the soil, in the tragic clash
of the saturated blue and green shades, Van Gogh expressed his dreams
of freedom and harmony in art somewhat darkened by a sense
of impossibility to realize these aims.

219
PAUL GAUGUIN (1848–1903)
Sunflowers. 1901
Oil on canvas. 72 x 91 cm. Acquired 1931
from the Museum of New Western Art
in Moscow; formerly the S. I. Shchukin
collection in Moscow

This latest of the Hermitage
paintings by Gauguin, created at
Dominique Island where the artist
moved from Tahiti, is filled with
mysticism and mystery. Among the
large yellow flowers there emerges
a widely open eye — the mysterious
All-Seeing Eye, and the immobile
face is reminiscent of the Buddha's
likeness. Christian artists depicted
the All-Seeing Eye encircled by
rays of sunlight, and the sunflower
is a well-known symbol of the Sun.
Did Gauguin associate his picture
with Christian symbolism? Its
subject matter is merely suggestive
of such interpretation, yet it does
not give any direct answer.

220
PAUL GAUGUIN (1848–1903)
Woman Holding a Fruit. 1893
Oil on canvas. 92 x 73 cm
Acquired 1948 from the Pushkin Museum
of Fine Art in Moscow;
formerly the I. A. Morozov collection
in Moscow

The heroine of this painting expresses Gauguin's
ideal of beauty. Her face is quiet, her features
are immobile. She looks like a statue carved
of a warm golden-coloured wood and
at the same time she is an alive and integral
part of her natural environment.
The contours outlining the figure of the woman
echo in the rhythms of the tree branches,
in the patterns of the skirt and in the spots
on the earth concentrating
in the pumpkin she holds in her hands,
which becomes the focal point of the entire
composition.

221
PAUL GAUGUIN (1848–1903)
Pastorales Tahitiennes. 1893
Oil on canvas. 86 x 113 cm
Acquired 1948 from the Museum
of New Western Art in Moscow; formerly the I. A. Morozov
collection in Moscow

Driven by a romantic striving to set himself free from the rigid
framework of European art, Gauguin found his "Golden Age"
at Tahiti Island. There, amidst the beautiful exotic scenery
and naïve aborigines living at one with nature,
the artist created in his pictures a fascinating world of dreams
and recollections. The canvas *Pastorales Tahitiennes*
is saturated with a musical quality which can be sensed
in the rhythm of the twisting trees and flowers and in the soft
movements of the Tahitian women.
The bright pure colours of the painting suggest a resemblance
to mediaeval enamels.

222
HENRI MATISSE (1869–1954)
The Dance. 1910
Oil on canvas. 260 x 391 cm. Acquired 1948 from the Museum
of New Western Art in Moscow;
formerly the S. I. Shchukin
collection in Moscow

Matisse painted two decorative panels,
The Dance and *Music*, for Sergei Shchukin's mansion in Moscow.
However, the painter endowed his decorative work with
a more profound symbolic meaning. In his words,
he painted the canvas with such a degree of intensity that would
make the idea of colour fully revealed — blue for the sky,
red for naked human bodies dancing under the sun
and green for nature.

223
Henri Matisse (1869–1954)
The Red Room (Dessert. Harmony in Red). 1908
Oil on canvas. 180 x 220 cm. Acquired 1948 from the Museum
of New Western Art in Moscow;
formerly the S. I. Shchukin
collection in Moscow

The Red Room can be compared with a concerto for a solo
instrument and orchestra where the main part is performed
by red colour. Originally the predominant colour
of the picture was blue and it was called *Harmony in Blue*,
but later, when his work had already been purchased
by Shchukin, Matisse transformed
it into *Harmony in Red*.

224
HENRI MATISSE (1869–1954)
Conversation. 1909
Oil on canvas. 177 x 217 cm
Acquired 1930 from the Museum of New Western Art
in Moscow; formerly the S. I. Shchukin
collection in Moscow

In this large-scale composition Matisse portrayed himself and his
wife Amélie. Although the artist denied that he had set for himself
the task of painting a portrait, nonetheless there is a kind
of dialogue based on the juxtaposition of the two strong
personalities, the two conventional
but strikingly lifelike figures standing against
the blue plane of the background.

225 ▼

Pablo Picasso (1881–1973)
The Visit (Two Sisters). 1902
Oil on canvas mounted on panel. 152 x 100 cm
Acquired 1948 from the Museum
of New Western Art in Moscow;
formerly the S. I. Shchukin
collection in Moscow

One of Picasso's best works from the Blue
Period, this painting was created by the artist
on the basis of real impressions and numerous
sketches from life. During the early period of his
life in Paris Picasso, then twenty-one-year old,
preferred to find characters for his work among
miserable and poor people. But real characters
have lost their concrete features in the painting.
Picasso's heroines are symbols of solitude
and suffering in the alien world filled
with a cold blue colour.

226
Pablo Picasso (1881–1973)
Lady with a Fan (After the Ball). 1908
Oil on canvas. 150 x 100 cm
Acquired 1934 from the Museum
of New Western Art in Moscow;
formerly the S. I. Shchukin
collection in Moscow

In 1906 Picasso arrived at the new painterly
system which later took shape under the name
of Cubism. The artist seems to construct
his characters of crudely hewn geometrical
forms without, however, depriving
them of human emotions.
The posture of his Cubist *Woman with a Fan*
is absolutely natural – she is seated in an armchair,
tired and relaxed; her head is drooping and her
hand seems to hold the light fan
with difficulty.

227
WASSILY KANDINSKY (1866–1944)
Composition No 6. 1913
Oil on canvas. 194 x 294 cm
Acquired 1948 from the Museum
of New Western Art in Moscow

Kandinsky, the founder of Abstract Expressionism,
is a major figure in twentieth-century world art.
His *Composition No 6*,
painted in Munich, is rightly regarded
as one of the artist's best works.
In his opinion, the composition is the highest
form of creative movement, a new reality
which is not connected
with the objective world and is perceived
only emotionally.

WASSILY KANDINSKY
(1866–1944)
Winter. 1909
Oil on canvas. 70 x 97 cm
Acquired 1948 from the Museum
of New Western Art in Moscow

At Murnau, Kandinsky worked
much out of doors, gradually
discarding the direct recording
of the motif in favour of
a greater generalization and
abstracting of natural forms.
In his *Winter* objects look like
flat colour spots, but the artist
has not yet broken with real
impressions — the vertical
rhythm of black lines is
reminiscent of bare dark tree-
trunks standing out clearly
against the background
of snow-bound hills.

229
WASSILY KANDINSKY
(1866–1944)
View at Murnau. 1908
Oil on canvas. 33 x 44 cm
Acquired 1948 from the Museum
of New Western Art in Moscow

In 1902 Kandinsky came
to Munich where he was going
to continue his studies in the
workshop of the well-known
German painter Franz von
Stuck famous as a teacher.
There he met Gabriel Munther
who soon became his wife.
They used to spend each
summer in a small village
of Murnau in the Alps,
one of the most picturesque
spots in Germany which
had attracted artists since
the beginning of the twentieth
century.

230

KARL FRIEDRICH LESSING (1808–1880)
*The Royal Couple Mourning the Death
of Their Daughter.* 1830
Oil on canvas. 215 x 193 cm. Acquired 1928 from
the Ropsha Palace near Leningrad

Lessing was an eminent representative of the
Düsseldorf school. He produced this painting at the
age of twenty-two. Its subject may have been taken
from the ballad *The Castle on the Water*
by the Romantic poet Uhland, which tells about
the sorrow of the parents who have lost
their only daughter.

231

FRANZ VON STUCK (1863–1928)
Fight for a Woman. 1905
Oil on panel. 90 x 117 cm
Acquired 1948 from the Museum of New Western Art in Moscow;
formerly the M. P. Riabushinsky
collection in Moscow

Stuck was an eminent representative of German Symbolism,
a founder of the Munich Sezession and a talented teacher
at the Academy of Arts where many outstanding artists,
including Wassily Kandinsky, were trained.
The subject of this picture was popular in the late nineteenth
century when the ideas of Friedrich Nietzsche exerted a strong
influence on German society.

◀ 232
AUGUSTE RODIN (1840–1917)
The Poet and His Muse. 1905
Marble. Acquired 1923 from
the Yeliseyev family collection

Rodin has much in common
with the Impressionists.
His manner is remarkable for
a heightened sense of plasticity
and dynamism. The changing
character of the world can be
felt in his marble groups
no less than in paintings by
Monet or Renoir. At the same
time, however, Rodin's pieces
are permeated with symbolism. In his *Poet and His Muse*
the sculptor personified the
idea about femininity inspiring
an artist. That is why the poet
leaning to his muse, is not
only dreaming but increasing
his creative power.

233 ▶
AUGUSTE RODIN (1840–1917)
Romeo and Juliet. 1905
Marble. Acquired 1923 from the Yeliseyev
family collection

Rodin always had difficulties with finding titles
for his statues. His works neither lose
nor acquire anything depending on whether
they feature literary or mythological
characters. Lovers clasped
in each other's arms – this subject might
be considered worthy of a sculptor's attention
in any age.
The hint of a balustrade in this sculptural
version of *Romeo and Juliet* probably suggests
Italy of the Renaissance period.

234

AUGUSTE RODIN (1840–1917)
Eternal Spring. 1905
Marble. Acquired 1923 from
the Yeliseyev family collection

A device of juxtaposing
smoothly polished surfaces
to rough, almost untreated
material was borrowed by
Rodin from Michelangelo,
but in Rodin's case it has
a profound symbolic message.
The rock from which beautiful
bodies seem to be born,
is a spatial and temporal
medium with no beginning
or end rather than a concrete
image. But true eternity is still
expressed in the beauty of
the human body and feelings.

THE HERMITAGE: A MUSEUM OF WORLD CULTURE

**Statue of the goddess
Sekhmet from the Mut temple
in Thebes. 15th century B.C.**
Egypt. Height 200 cm. Granite

**Pile carpet
Pazyryk Barrow
(The Mountain Altai)
5th–4th century B.C.**
Persia. 200 x 185 cm. Wool

Almost immediately after the revolution, the Hermitage began tackling the problem of reorganization and becoming a truly modern twentieth-century museum. From the outset the Hermitage had been a repository not only of Western European and Ancient works that were the main objects of collection in the eighteenth and nineteenth centuries, but also items of non-European origin: Slavic and Early Russian antiquities, exotic Eastern articles, Russian silver, porcelain, and much else besides. These items were few in number and did not stand out from the general composition of the museum collections. By the early twentieth century, however, the material belonging to the distinctive cultures of the Orient, Russia and the primitive world called out for more appropriate treatment and intensive study. In the first half of the twentieth century, the three departments that had formed historically in the Hermitage – Western European, Ancient Art and Numismatics – were joined by three others responsible for the East, Archaeology and the History of Russian Culture.

This process applied above all to articles from the East. Many of them had come into the museum back in the eighteenth century, often by chance: Turkish and Persian arms presented to Peter the Great, carved gems from Ancient Egypt, Byzantium and China among Catherine II's glyptic collection and Eastern coins. In the 1830s, under Nicholas I, who devoted more attention to the Ancient World, the first artefacts from Ancient Egypt were purchased: sarcophagi, sculptural portraits, a granite effigy of the lion-headed goddess Sekhmet from the temple of Mut at Karnak. Thanks to the development of Russian studies of the Middle East and numerous expeditions to the area, by the turn of the twentieth century the Hermitage possessed collections of Coptic, Islamic, Sassanian and Byzantine art.

On 1 November 1920, on the initiative of outstanding Russian scholars in the field, a Department of the East was established in the Hermitage. It began with some 10,000 items collected by the museum before the revolution, but rapidly expanded. It absorbed a wealth of material from collections scattered around other Russian museums and repositories. In 1925 the Hermitage was given collections of Eastern applied art – ceramics, glass, bronze, Chinese porcelain, lacquerware and carved stone – from the museum of the Baron Stieglitz College of Industrial Design in Leningrad. A particularly valuable addition was the collection assembled by the noted Russian traveller Piotr Kozlov. In the early twentieth century he discovered and excavated the ancient city of Khara-Khoto that existed in the Gobi Desert between the eleventh and sixteenth centuries. It produced unique examples of Buddhist art, mainly numerous Tibeto-Tangut and Chinese religious images painted on canvas, paper and silk. Equally valuable for the new department was a collection of sculpture in loess and wall-paintings from the ancient Chinese monastery of Qian-Fuo-Dong ("The Cave of a Thousand Buddhas") collected back in the 1910s by Sergei Oldenburg's expedition. From the late 1920s onwards the department organised its own archaeological expeditions to the Caucasus and Central Asia. For almost three decades from 1939 excavations were conducted at Karmir-Blur hill in Armenia, uncovering the main city of Urartu, a kingdom that existed between the eighth and sixth centuries B.C., Expeditions, purchases made through the Expert Commission, official and private gifts from Eastern countries all considerably enlarged the department's collections. Today it is one of the world's largest collections of cultural artefacts and art of the peoples of the East. Its superb stocks reflect the culture of all regions of the East. Displays in the ground floor of the Winter Palace are devoted to the Ancient East – Egypt and a small collection from Western Asia. There too, on the Admiralty side, are displays of the art and culture of Central Asia. Here you can see unique wall-paintings from the ancient palaces of Pendjikent and Varakshi (7th–8th centuries A.D.), ceramics and tiles that adorned the mosque of Samarkand in the time of Tamerlane, and much more. On the second floor of the palace there are displays of the very rich collections from Byzantium, the Middle East (Iran, Syria, Turkey) and the Far East. There is a particular wealth of superb works of painting and sculpture and a host of extremely rare examples of the artistic crafts practised in China and Tibet.

Ten years after the Department of the East, in 1931, another new department – of Archaeology – was created. It brought together the art and artefacts of the Scythians and Sarmatians (7th century B.C. – 3rd century A.D.) that had been kept with works from the Classical World in the Department of

Antiquities and material relating to the culture of primitive peoples. After the revolution these had been expanded by private collections. The department began with almost 20,000 primitive artefacts. Soon however the collection was many times that size due to regular archaeological expeditions. The displays of this department, located on the ground floor of the Winter Palace, present unique items indicating how humanity lived in the remotest times: tools and the earliest-ever works of art from the Palaeolithic era, petroglyphs from the Neolithic age, early Bronze Age sculpture… World famous are the works of Scythian art and finds from the burial mounds of the Altai mountains that are unique in terms of both assortment and state of preservation. Finely-made items of felt, silk and wood were found preserved in permafrost in the graves of the nomadic Altai chieftains. They include the world's oldest Persian carpet dating from the fifth century B.C., found in the Pazyryk mound.

In April 1941 extremely rich stocks of Russian eighteenth- and nineteenth-century cultural artefacts were transferred to the Hermitage from the Ethnographic Museum in Leningrad. The items – furniture, porcelain, clothing and portraits from St Petersburg palaces and mansions left unattended, old Russian books, icons and mediaeval antiquities from private collections – had ended up in conditions unsuitable for their study or even preservation. The Hermitage at that time was the institution that could assume responsibility for this treasure. The Hermitage had long been a repository of precious Russian-made articles – table silver and porcelain, the court jewellery, superb furniture from the apartments of the Winter Palace, portraits of the imperial family… Now the museum recovered items that had once been in the Peter the Great Gallery of the Small Hermitage – belongings of the Tsar, lathes from his turnery, pieces made by the Tsar and his craftsmen, a walrus-ivory chandelier, a model of a triumphal column planned to mark Peter's victories over the Swedes. Accordingly, in 1941 a new department was created in the Hermitage. In post-war times it was enlarged with collections of old scientific devices and instruments, seventeenth- to twentieth-century Russian and captured enemy banners, historical documents and photographs. From 1954 onwards department staff continually went on expeditions to the Russian North, gathering a remarkably extensive and high-quality collection of Early Russian icons. The department's displays that were installed after the Second World War in the halls of the Winter Palace provide a panoramic view of many aspects of Russian cultural life as it developed from the early Middle Ages to the beginning of the twentieth century.

The Department of the History of Russian Culture is constantly growing. New sections and exhibitions are formed from its enormous stocks. In 1987–89 Hermitage specialists carried out radical restoration work on the Hermitage Theatre. On the lowest floor of the building they uncovered and reconstructed fragments of the old Winter Palace of Peter the Great – the Tsar's private rooms and the Large State Room – returning them to their historical appearance. Peter's personal belongings were installed in the rooms, recreating the setting in which the first Russian emperor and founder of St Petersburg died.

The Menshikov Palace is a branch of the Hermitage and the Department of the History of Russian Culture. The palace, located across the Neva on the embankment of Vasilyevsky Island, was built in 1710–20 for Alexander Menshikov, Peter the Great's companion from childhood who rose from humble beginnings to become the first governor of St Petersburg. Later, right through to the 1960s, it housed various educational institutions. In 1966 it was given to the Hermitage. After scholarly restoration the palace looks almost as it did under its first owner. Its interiors, where very rare early-eighteenth-century decor has survived, were given over to a display that presents the history of the palace, the culture and daily existence of Peter the Great's time.

The twentieth century made the Hermitage a tremendous museum of Russian and world culture and that is how it enters the twenty-first century.

Guhyasamaja – a Tantric guarding deity of the Buddhas
18th century
Tibet. Height 24 cm. Gilded bronze
Acquired 1934 from
the E.E. Ukhtomsky collection

Icon: *The Intercession*
16th century. From the
Church of the Intercession
in the village of Volnavolo,
Leningrad Region
Tempera on panel. 65 x 47 x 2.5 cm
Acquired 1955 by the Hermitage
expedition

235 ▲
Statue of Queen Arsinoë II
Egypt. The Late Kingdom. Basaltes

In 322 B.C. Egypt was conquered by the Greeks. Egyptian
sculptors of the Hellenistic period, trying to retain the
peculiar features of national sculpture, created in this
period idealized images following age-old traditions.
One of these is the statue of Arsinoë II holding
in her hand a cornucopia, representations
of which had been unknown in Egypt before
the invasion of the Greeks.

236 *(top right)*
Stele showing the royal economy manager
and fan bearer Ipi before God Anubis
First half of the 14th century B.C.
Memphis. The New Kingdom. Pained limestone. 72 x 51.5 cm

This funerary stele found in a tomb depicts its owner in
front of the jackal-headed god Anubis, patron of the
dead. Anubis holds the sign of life in his right hand and
the sceptre in the left. According to the canon adopted in
Egyptian art, the figures are portrayed in profile, with
their shoulders turned frontally. Man's subordinate
position with regard to the god is expressed in the fact
that even an official of high rank was invariably
represented in ancient Egyptian murals on a much
smaller scale than deities.

Dish. 7th–8th century
Iran. Diameter 28 cm. Silver-gilt
Found during excavations
in the village of Sludka, Perm
Province, in 1780. Acquired from
the Stroganov family collection
in St Petersburg

The Hermitage boasts
the world's largest collection
of Persian silverware of the
Sassanian period (more than
50 Sassanian items and about
60 items of the Sassanian
circle). These objects came
mainly from the hoards
unearthed in the Urals where
they had mainly been brought
in exchange for furs.

◀ **237**
Statuette of a man
15th century B.C.
Egypt. The New Kingdom. Wood

The figure of a man is shown
in the pose traditional for
ancient Egyptian sculpture –
the body is straight, the left
feet seems to make a step
forward, the arms are put
down, yet with all its
conventionality and rigidity,
there is a plastic freedom
and a sort of elegance
in the image.

239
Jug. 11th century
Egypt. Rock crystal and silver

In the tenth century the powerful Fatimid
dynasty established firm positions in Egypt and
claimed themselves to be caliphs. Numerous
workshops owned by the caliphs produced
notable objects of applied art.
This jug of rock crystal is
a magnificent example dating from this period.
Its surface is decorated
with an elaborate ornamental design of two
lions which emphasizes the beauty of the
natural material.

241 ▼
The Buddha Amida Greeting the Soul
of the Righteous Man on the Way to the Pure Land
Khara-Khoto, Tibet. Natural colours on canvas. 99 x 63.8 cm
Found 1908–09 by the P. K. Kozlov expedition

Fine examples of Far Eastern culture of the twelfth and thirteenth centuries were discovered by Piotr Kozlov's expeditions of 1908–09 and 1926 to the ancient town of Khara-Khoto located at the border of the Gobi Desert. The town was the centre of the Tangut state which had emerged in Central Asia in the tenth century. After the town had become desolate in the thirteenth century it was gradually covered with sand. Therefore the discovered objects – beautiful wood engravings and paintings on paper, silk and canvas – which laid without access of air had an excellent state of preservation. This artistically beautiful icon shows the Buddha on two lotuses. The two Bodhisattvas holding lotus flowers, a Buddhist symbol of purity, suggest to the soul of a righteous man to step on it as on the "pure earth, unstained by sins". The righteous man himself is depicted in the lower right-hand corner of the elaborate composition. The space around the figures is filled with representations of idiophonous musical instruments.

240 ▲
Head of the Buddha. 8th century
Tunhuang, China. The Tang Dynasty. Painted clay
Found 1914–15 by the expedition
of Academician Sergei Oldenburg

This image comes from an outstanding centre of mediaeval China – the monastery of Qian-Fuo-Dong
(the "Cave of a Thousand Buddhas").
It was discovered by a St Petersburg scholar, Academician Sergei Oldenburg,
near Tunhuang, a city which had once stood at the starting point of the Silk Route.
The walls of the monastery caves preserved fine examples of wall painting as well as pieces of monumental sculpture produced of soft and porous loess clay. The Tang period was the time of flowering of Chinese culture which saw the spread of porcelain and the introduction of paper and book-printing.
Buddhism, which had penetrated to China through the Sinkiang district
in the first century A.D., exerted a strong influence on the development
of Chinese art.

242
*Medician Buddh*a
Natural paints on canvas
Discovered 1908–09
by the Piotr Kozlov expedition
at Khara-Khoto in Tibet

The Buddha of healing is
shown seated in the traditional
lotus attitude wearing a red
garment stylized in imitation
of a monk's patchwork dress.
He holds in his hand his
permanent attribute –
a bowl with *maribolana* fruits.
Next to the Buddha are two
Bodhisattvas – the white one
with a symbol of the moon
and the body-coloured one
with a symbol of the sun.
Totally the composition
comprises thirty-nine figures
including seven related
Buddhas, located in the upper
part of the picture, as well as
various Hindu and Buddhist
deities.

243
The Rotunda
By Auguste de Montferrand
(1786–1858)
(Room 156)

There was no such room in
the eighteenth century. After
the living apartments had been
reconstructed, a dark square
room formed at the joint of
northern and western blocks of
the Winter Palace. Montferrand
redesigned it into a circular hall
lit from above and reminiscent
of round ancient temples (hence
the name of the interior). In the
centre of the hall, now part
of the Department of Russian
Culture, is displayed a model
of the triumphal column
created by the sculptor Carlo
Bartolomeo Rastrelli in honour
of the victory of the Russian
troops over the Swedes in the
Northern War.

244, 245
The Concert Hall
By Vasily Stasov
Detal *(Room 152)*

One of the main state rooms
of the Neva enfilade running
along the Neva, this hall
was conceived by Giacomo
Quarenghi in the late
eighteenth century, but after
the fire of 1837 it was
redesigned by Vasily Stasov
who largely preserved
Quarenghi's composition.
He altered only the colour
scheme – the hall, once faced
with coloured artificial marble
became white. Burnt statues
were replaced with figures of
the ancient Muses and deities.
Today the hall is used
as the venue for temporary
exhibitions. In the centre of
it stands the decorative tomb
of St Alexander Nevsky.

248 ▶

Icon: *The Last Judgement*
First half of the 16th century
The Novgorod school
Tempera on panel. 163 x 118 x 3 cm
From the Church of St Nicholas (1763), village of Nionoksa,
Belomorsk District, Archangel Region. Acquired 1960
through the Hermitage expedition

This monumental icon was executed according
to the best traditions of the Novgorod school –
the bright red, blue and yellow colours give
it a festive air despite of the austerity and deep
significance of its subject.
The composition looks almost mathematically
balanced and is divided in a series
of semicircular tiers.
In the upper part of the icon the Angels
are unfolding a scroll with a representation
of the sun, moon and stars over Christ seated
on the throne and judging the souls
of human beings. Next to Him are
the figures of the Virgin and the Apostles
while below is a tier with people coming
to the Last Judgement.
The composition completes with a depiction
of weighing the souls and the scenes
of Hell and Paradise.

246
Icon: *St Nicholas*
Late 15th – early 16th century
The Northern school. Tempera on panel. 72 x 51.5 x 3 cm
From the Church of the Intercession (18th-century),
Liadiny pogost, Kargopol District, Archangel Region
Acquired 1957 through the Hermitage expedition

St Nicholas was one of the most popular saints
in Russia. The unknown northern icon-painter
depicts the saint in episcopal vestments,
with the Gospel in his left hand, and blessing
believers with the right.

247
Icon: *The Miracle of St George*
Late 15th – early 16th century
The Northern school. Tempera on panel. 57 x 43 x 2.5 cm
From the Chapel of St George (1779), village of Niormushi
on the Onega River, Plesetsk District, Archangel Region
Acquired 1959 through the Hermitage expedition

The anonymous icon-painter active in Archangel
depicted St George as a warrior mounted on
a white horse and striking a dragon with his
spear. St George personified in Russia a victory
over the powers of darkness and was revered as
the patron of the autocracy, soldiers and peasants.

249
IVAN NIKITIN (CA 1680–1742)
Portrait of Elizabeth Petrovna as a Child. 1712
Oil on canvas. 54 x 43 cm
Acquired 1941 from the State Museum Expedition;
formerly the Gorchakov family collection

Elizabeth (1709–1761), daughter of Peter the
Great and Catherine I, the Russian Empress from
1741 to 1761, is shown in the portrait as
a three-year-old girl. Nikitin was a talented artist
sent by Peter the Great to improve his knowledge
abroad. After several years of training in Italy,
he became the leading portrait painter
of this period. Nikitin's portrait of Elizabeth
is his earliest surviving work.

250 ▶
CARL LUDWIG JOHANN CHRISTINECK
(1730/32 – NOT LATER THAN 1794)
*Portrait of Count Alexei Bobrinsky
as a Boy.* 1769
Oil on canvas. 90 x 73.5 cm
Acquired 1941 from the State Museum Expedition;
formerly the A. A. Bobrinsky collection in St Petersburg

Count Alexei Grigoryevich Bobrinsky (1772–1813)
was an illegitimate child of Catherine the Great and
Count Grigory Orlov. Brought up in the family of
Ivan Betskoi, President of the Academy of Arts, he
then graduated from the Free Cadet Corps and stayed
in Paris for several years. On returning to Russia
he settled on his estate in Tula Province and engaged
mainly in agricultural pursuits revealing also an
interest in mineralogy.

Portrait of Catherine the Great in a Travelling Costume. Ca 1787
BY AN UNKNOWN ARTIST ACTIVE IN THE SECOND HALF OF THE 18TH CENTURY
Oil on canvas. 52.5 x 65.8 cm

There exists an extensive iconography of Catherine the Great. She encouraged artists for the creation of her portraits but as a rule they are formal likenesses. The present half-length portrait showing Catherine the Great in her travelling costume is remarkable for its individual character and lack of idealization. It was probably painted by the serf painter of Grigory Potemkin in Kiev, where the Empress stayed during her travel to the Crimea. Catherine undertook such a long travel from St Petersburg in order to see her new possessions – the lands of the Crimea, formerly owned by Turkey, captured for Russia by Potemkin. Legend has it that in order to conceal from the Empress the poverty and desolation of the Russian villages which she could see on her way from the carriage, Potemkin ordered to set up along the road painted decorations featuring rich and splendid houses. Similar ostentatious projects have been known since as "Potemkin's villages".

252
IVAN VISHNIAKOV (1699–1761)
Portrait of Stepanida Yakovleva. After 1756
Oil on canvas. 90 x 72 cm
Acquired 1941 from the State Museum Expedition;
before 1928 in the A. N. Yakovleva collection

This portrait of Stepanida Yakovleva is a companion piece to a portrait of her husband, Mikhail Yakovlev, son of an eminent St Petersburg tax-farmer, who owned several plants in the Urals and received the title of a gentleman in 1761. In keeping with the Russian tradition, the artist lovingly and carefully paints out flower patterns and laces on the dress of the simple round-faced young woman who does not yet feel at ease in the role of a rich St Petersburg lady.

260 ▶
**The Dining-Room in the Winter Palace
of Peter the Great**

The rooms of the third and last Winter Palace
of Peter the Great, partly destroyed
during the construction of the Hermitage Theatre,
have reached us without inner decoration.
Their former designation is unknown.
After restoration the Dining-Room has been
furnished in keeping with the fashion
of the Petrine age. The sealed bottle of wine was
found among construction rubble during
restoration.

◀ 258
The carriage of Peter the Great. Early 1720s
Elm, oak, pine, leather, velvet and metal

This carriage intended for entertainment rides
was produced shortly before the death of Peter
the Great from drawings by Nicholas
Pineau. There are only two vehicles of this type
in Russia now.

**259
Wax effigy of Peter
the Great. 1725
BY CARLO BARTOLOMEO
RASTRELLI (1677–1744)**
Wax and wood

The posthumous wax effigy,
or "wax person" as it was called,
was produced by the sculptor
Rastrelli at the will of Empress
Catherine I. Right after the
death of the Tsar the sculptor
took a wax mask from his
face, made casts of his hands
and feet. The completed work
presented a faithful copy
of the outward appearance
and stature of Peter the Great
who was 2.04 metres (6 feet
7 inches) tall. Notably, the effigy
was made in wood and only
the hands, feet and face were
of wax. All the things put on
the Tsar's figure – the formal
costume embroidered with
silver, the order of St Andrew
the First-Called with a red
order ribbon, shoes and
even the wig – are authentic.
Today, the wax effigy is
displayed in the Palace of Peter
the Great recreated under the
building of the Hermitage
Theatre.

261
The Menshikov Palace
BY GIOVANNI MARIO FONTANA (1670–?)
AND JOHANN GOTTFRIED SCHÄDEL (1680s–1752)

The Menshikov Palace, a landmark of Petrine
architecture, one of the first stone buildings
in St Petersburg, became the property
of the Hermitage in 1977. Today it is a branch
of the Department of the History of Russian
Culture.

262
UNKNOWN 18TH-CENTURY ARTIST
Portrait of Prince Alexander Menshikov
1716–20
Oil on canvas

Alexander Menshikov (1673–1729) was a major
state and military figure of the age of Peter
the Great. After the death of the Tsar his closest
associate was accused of contriving a coup
and exiled to Siberia.

263
The Menshikov Palace. The Walnut Study. 1717
By Giovannni Mario Fontana (1670–?)

The palace of Prince Alexander Menshikov was the first large-scale edifice put up
in the newly built capital of Russia. Menshikov, the first governor of St Petersburg, amassed
in his palace a beautiful collection of painting, sculpture and applied art.
After the omnipotent official was dismissed and exiled, these treasures enriched the Imperial
art collections. We do not know for sure the name of the architect responsible for the
construction of the Menshikov Palace. Most of scholars believe that it was built by Giovanni
Mario Fontana who came to Russia in 1703. The design of the palace was strictly symmetrical.
Walnut panels adorned with inlaid decoration and gilded carving.
This is one of a few rooms in the palace which has completely retained its initial decoration.
The extensive, light interiors designed as a suite of state rooms were adorned with different
materials such as Dutch tiles and various kinds of precious wood. The owner's study located
in the south-eastern projection of the building was also known as
the Walnut Study because it was panelled with walnut rarely used in that period.
The warm tone of the natural wood covering the walls from top to bottom is highlighted
by gilding and inlaid decoration. The painted ceiling decoration and the tile stove in the corner
of the study complete the exquisite and lavish decor of the room.

STEPPING INTO THE FUTURE: ENTERING THE 21ST CENTURY

T

he twentieth century is at an end. One more era in the history of the Hermitage is passing away, but even today, the museum is writing a new page in its history. Despite all the economic and political difficulties in Russia, from the middle of the 1980s the Hermitage has been engaged in a long-term programme of development. It is oriented to the future; its goal is to radically update the old museum, fitting it to meet tomorrow's demands.

First and foremost, the museum is seeking to make new, creative use of what has been accumulated and created over the almost two-and-a-half centuries of its existence. Restoration and reconstruction of the old buildings has begun. New lighting and air-conditioning is being installed in the halls. A new entrance from Palace Square is being created through the courtyard-garden. The historical interiors are being renewed: the throne area in the St George Hall is being recreated; the portraits of members of the ruling dynasty that before the revolution hung in the Romanov Gallery of the Small Hermitage have returned to the walls in one of the rooms.

Forgotten traditions are being revived: the Large Throne Room is once again the setting for official ceremonies, now relating to the museum: here awards are made to distinguished members of staff on St George's Day; historical and artistic relics returning to the Hermitage are formally received. The Hermitage Theatre is used for stage performances and concerts as in Catherine's day. The Academy of Music created in the Hermitage and concerts by the Hermitage symphony orchestra in the museum halls are a first step towards the cultural centre that the Hermitage is becoming.

Palace Square.
The Alexander Column
ARCHITECT AUGUSTE
DE MONTFERRAND. 1834
The General Staff building
ARCHITECT CARLO ROSSI
1820–27

The Coiling Panther
Siberia, the Asian part
of Scythia
Gold. 7th–6th century B.C.
Acquired 1859 from the Siberian
Collection of Peter the Great

Another step into the future was the formal opening in 1998 of the "Golden Treasury". The modernization of old displays and the creation of new ones is among the Hermitage's main tasks as the new century approaches. The new Golden Treasury was constructed in the inner apartments of the Winter Palace and equipped with the latest lighting, ventilation and temperature-control systems and a complex alarm system. The state-of-the-art display cases contain Ancient Greek and Scythian gold and precious items from the East. These are old Hermitage collections. The first ancient gold articles belonged to Peter the Great: jewellery of the ancient nomads of Siberia, presented to the Tsar by Nikita Demidov, the Ural industrialist, in 1718. In the 1830s archaeological work began in the south of Russia – in the Crimea, the steppes around the Sea of Azov, the Northern Caucasus and the Dnieper basin. In ancient times those areas had been home to both Greeks, who built cities and states on the shores of the Black and Azov Seas, and nomadic tribes, the most notable of which were the Scythians (7th–3rd century B.C.). Excavation of the now-famous Scythian burial mounds yielded a host of precious golden ornaments. They include unique masterpieces of the Scythians' Animal Style, such as the world-renowned plaques in the form of a deer and a panther, as well as magnificent examples of Ancient Greek metalwork and jewellery. Many Greek artefacts were decorated with images of Scythians created in the best traditions of classical Greek art. The Eastern collection consists of diplomatic gifts to the Russian rulers, archaeological or chance finds, and purchases made at various times and includes artefacts of gold and precious stones from India, China and Iran. In the new Golden Treasury all these collections are combined for the first time in a single display. Together they demonstrate the development and achievements of the jeweller's art on a world scale, from Classical antiquity and the age of the nomads to the work of the mediaeval East.

This is just the first in a whole set of new displays being developed by the "Gallery of Jewellery", a new element in the structure of the Hermitage, set up in 1999. The name of a display that existed in the nineteenth-century museum (in one of the galleries of the Small Hermitage) has been given to a subdivision that brings together all the Hermitage collection of jewellery – the extremely rich collections of Western European and Russian works as well. Those go back to Catherine II's "Diamond Apartment". The clocks and bouquets of precious stones belonging to Empress Elizabeth, the exquisite dressing-cases and diamond-studded snuff-boxes of Catherine herself were later joined by pieces created by celebrated

The exhibition hall
in the General Staff building.
The Dining-Room in
the former state apartments
of the Minister of Foreign
Affairs Karl Nesselrode
ARCHITECT CARLO ROSSI
1820–27

European and Russian jewellers of the nineteenth and early twentieth centuries. Particularly renowned are the works that the Fabergé company created for the court.

As the new century dawns, the Hermitage is striving to fill the gaps in its collections. The most significant of these formed when, for a long time after 1917, the museum was unable to buy contemporary Western works of art. Only in the late 1970s and 1980s, through the gifts of collectors and artists, did it acquire individual works from the 1930s–80s – notably by Matisse (previously represented only by pre-1917 paintings), the American Rockwell Kent and the Italian Guttuso. The museum even managed to form a small section of twentieth-century Italian sculpture from works donated by Manzú, Messina, Greco and Morero. These were, however, random acquisitions and the Hermitage lacks works by leading figures of that significant portion of the century when Russia was cut off from the wider art world. At the very end of the century, though, in 1997–98, the Hermitage again returned to world art market and purchased at an international auction several works by twentieth-century artists – Soutine, Dufy, Rouault, Utrillo and Jawlensky.

The main, decisive step for the museum in the new century will be the creation of the "Great Hermitage". This project envisages the transfer to the Hermitage of several buildings adjoining Palace Square. They will be linked with the old museum buildings in a single complex. This is the largest museum project in Russia for the past hundred years, and implementation of it has already begun. In the 1990s the Hermitage embarked on the reconstruction of the east wing of the General Staff building after it was handed over to the museum. This magnificent edifice, originally built by Carlo Rossi in 1820–27, forms a mighty arc enclosing the south side of Palace Square.

Its two wings are linked by an arch crowned by a monumental chariot of Glory, a symbol of Russia's triumph. In the nineteenth century the east wing contained the Foreign Ministry – offices and the living apartments of the minister, Count Nesselrode, who from 1828 was Chancellor of the Russian Empire. It was for him that Rossi designed the suite of state rooms and private apartments. We can still admire the exquisite painting and grisaille work on the walls and ceilings; ornamental mouldings, mirrors and patterned parquet floors. In these genuine elegant interiors in the manner of Alexandrine Classicism, as the French Empire style is customarily known in Russia, an exhibition of art from the age of two emperors – Alexander I and Napoleon Bonaparte – has been opened under the title "Beneath the Sign of the Eagle" For the first time the Hermitage was able to present on such scale and in such fullness its magnificent collection of early-nineteenth-century French and Russian applied art.

CHAÏM SOUTINE (1893–1944)
Self-Portrait
with the Beard. 1916
France. Oil on canvas. 54 x 30.5 cm
1916. Acquired 1997 in accordance
with a decree of the President
of the Russian Federation
on the enrichment of the collections
of the State Hermitage

For the first time too, a permanent place was found here for two unique series of decorative paintings – Maurice Denis's *Story of Psyche* and Pierre Bonnard's *Mediterranean Sea*. Created at the turn of the twentieth century for the mansion of the noted Muscovite collectors Ivan Morozov, these paintings entered the Hermitage back in 1948. They were shown only in temporary exhibitions as the rooms used for the permanent display of French art were too low to take them. The panels by Denis and Bonnard in the General Staff building is a first step towards the creation of a whole new display of the world-famous Shchukin and Morozov collections that will be moved there from the Winter Palace.

In the future this building will also be used for the display of items from the museum stocks for which there was never enough room in the old premises porcelain, tapestries, furniture, clocks, arms and armour, banners and clothing. The displays of art in the Great Hermitage will become the core of a multifunctional museum space with centres of artistic education and cultural leisure, incorporating exhibition galleries, lecture halls, a theatre and concert salons, libraries and media facilities, a computer information centre, book and antiques shops, cafés, restaurants and much more.

To become a great twenty-first-century museum, equipped to the latest standards, a centre of culture and a place where people can experience first-hand the riches of the world's artistic heritage – that is the task on which the Hermitage is engaged as it moves into the twenty-first century.

264
Bowl. 4th century B.C.
The Kul-Oba Barrow. Gold
Found 1830 by P. Dubrux

This golden bowl of Greek work has a magnificent
engraving on its reverse side. The opening in the
middle was intended for supporting the bowl with
a thumb. The bowl bears representations of real
and fantastic creatures arranged along its body –
the centre of the composition is encircled with a
chain of dolphins, then follows a pattern of Gorgon
heads having haircuts in the shape of snakes
and bearded Silenuses. Small relief representations
of bees compete the ornament.

265
Deer. 7th–6th century B.C.
The Kostromskaya Station Barrow
Gold. Found 1897 by R. I. Veselovsky

The Hermitage's outstanding
collection of Scythian golden
articles found during
excavations in the south of
Russia, is preserved in the
Special Gold Room. This golden
shield decoration, a masterpiece of the Scythian "Animal
Style", strikes us by its perfect
execution and expressive pose
of the deer captured during a
jump, with its neck stretched
out and its legs pressed to the
body. Specialists assume that
the image of deer had a magic
significance associated with
the sun and eternal life.

266 ▶
Comb. 4th century B.C.
The Solokha Barrow. Height 12.3 cm,
width 10.2 cm. Gold
Found 1912–13 by the N. N. Veselovsky
expedition in the Dnieper area

This comb, evidently created
by a Greek craftsman for
a Scythian leader, reminds
the austere classical façade
of a Greek temple. Its long,
four-edged teeth play the part
of columns supporting a frieze
of lions on which seemingly
rests a pediment with the
figures of fighting Scythian
warriors. The warriors, horses
and lions welded of two
chased halves of plaques are
depicted with a striking
mastery characteristic of Greek
jewellers.

◀ 267
**Vessel with representations
of Scythians. 4th century B.C.**
The Kul-Oba Barrow. Gold
Found 1830 by P. Dubrux

This is a fine example of Greek
work featuring Scythians
in their characteristic wide
trousers and long jackets
uncommon for the Greek eye.
Also unusual for the Greeks
were the nomads' long hair
and pointed hats. Probably
the vessel depicts some of the
Scythians' plentiful magic rites.

269 ▶
Temple pendants
4th century B.C.
The Bolshaya Bliznitsa Barrow,
Northern Black Sea Coast
Gold, chased and engraved

Usually such pendants in the characteristic
disc form with amphora-like details
suspended by chains were attached to
a woman's temples as part of an elaborate
and rich set of golden jewellery.

◀ 268

Amphora. 4th century B.C.
The Chertomlyk Barrow
Height 75 cm. Silver, chased and gilded
Found 1863 by the I. E. Zabelin
expedition in the Dnieper area
(near Nikopol)

This Greek silver vessel for wine, a piece
of perfect form and elegant work, was
discovered in a Scythian barrow. Judging
from the character of the representations
on the shoulders and body of the vase,
it was commissioned for a Scythian leader.
The upper part of the vessel features the
figures of Scythians hobbling wild horses.
The three taps for wine are shaped like
the heads of a winged horse and lions,
the animals worshipped by the Scythians.

270
Ear-ring (one of a pair)
4th century B.C.
Found 1853 in a barrow near Theodosia
Gold, chased, engraved and cast, microtechnique

This set of ear-rings, unearthed during excavations of a rich Greek
woman's burial mound near Theodosia, is a masterpiece
of Greek jewellery. The process of its manufacture involved
uniquely complex microtechnical operations.
Attached to the disc is a crescent-shaped detail decorated
with four horses and a chariot driven by Apollo.
The crescent itself consists of tiny balls welded together to form
lozenge shapes, each composed of four golden grains.

271
Scent bottle. 17th century
India. Gold, rubies and emeralds

This piece of jewellery comes from the legendary
treasury of the Great Moguls who ruled India
in the sixteenth and seventeenth centuries.
The treasury was plundered in 1730 by the
Iranian ruler Nadir Shah, who sent the scent
bottle, among other objects, as a present to
the Russian Empress Anna Ioannovna.

◄ 272
Bouquet of gems in a glass vessel
Late 1750s
BY LOUIS DAVID DUVAL

Only a few precious objects of this kind
have reached us. In the centre of the bouquet
which apparently served as a piece of
decoration, is a huge, skilfully worked
amethyst in the form of tulip surrounded
with tiny diamonds. The decoration
of the bouquet includes rubies, emeralds,
Dutch topazes, pyropes, spinels,
aquamarines and turquoises.

273 ►
Nécessaire or toilet set. 18th century. England
Gold, agate and diamonds

Toilet sets, boxes filled with various objects –
miniature appliances, thimbles, scissors,
carnets (small notebooks with golden pencils),
and even a special utensil for cleaning
ears – were fashionable decorations
of lady's toilet tables.

◄ 274
Model of the Tsar's Regalia. 1900
BY CARL FABERGÉ (1846–1920)
Gold, diamonds, pearls, sapphire
and spinels

The famous St Petersburg jeweller produced, specially
for the World Exhibition in Paris, a copy
of the royal regalia which had been made for Empress Catherine
the Great by the court jeweller Jerèmie Posier in the second half
of the eighteenth century.
The copy of the regalia, reduced ten times,
consist of the large crown decorated with diamonds and spinels,
the scepter crowned with the unique Orlov diamond,
one of the largest gems in the world, and the small crown.
Fabergé's copy won in Paris the Large Prize
and the Large Gold Medal, and the jeweller himself received
the title of the best European master.

277 ▶
Bouquet:
Cornflowers and Oats
Early 20th century
By Carl Fabergé (1846–1920)
Silver, enamel and rock crystal

Bouquets created by Fabergé in the fashion of famous eighteenth-century bouquets of precious stones, became fashionable decorations of rich drawing-rooms. They were marked by great elegance combined with simplicity.

275
Doorbell push-buttons. Early 1900s
By Carl Fabergé (1846–1920)
St Petersburg
Silver, guilloché enamels

Fabergé's workshop in St Petersburg produced not only unique priceless jewellery, but also quite accessible objects of everyday use – frames for photographs, cigarette-cases, tobacco-boxes, statuettes of semiprecious stones and even push-buttons for electric doorbells. Fabergé liked to coat metal surfaces with several layers of semitransparent enamels.

276
Cigarette-case and powder-case. Early 1900s
By Carl Fabergé (1846–1920)
St Petersburg
Silver, guilloché enamels

The technique of enamel work used by Fabérge for the decoration of articles was very complex. The silver or gold base was covered with engraving. The enamel which was applied in several layers on the surface of the metal was transparent and therefore the engraving (the so-called *guilloché* background) could be seen.

279
RAOUL DUFY (1877–1953)
*Regatta (Sail-Boats in
the Dauville Harbour). Ca* 1936
Oil on canvas. 54 x 80.8 cm
Acquired 1998 by the Hermitage
Purchasing Committee in Paris

This is the Hermitage's first
work by the eminent French
master who once participated,
together with Matisse,
in Fauvist exhibitions.
The painting was not widely
known as it was in a private
collection. Meanwhile its
artistic merits are very high.

◀ **278**
GIACOMO MANZÙ (1908–1990)
Tebe Seated. 1983
Bronze. The artist's gift of 1986

This statue, together with
his painting *The Artist and His
Model*, which serves as a background for the sculpture, was
presented to the Hermitage
by the famous Italian sculptor.

280
GEORGES ROUAULT (1878–1958)
The Head of Christ. Ca 1939
Oil on paper mounted on canvas. 65 x 50 cm
Acquired 1998 by the Hermitage Purchasing
Committee in Paris

Rouault who began his creative career
with a participation in Fauvist
exhibitions, was sometimes mentioned
as a "French Expressionist". The artist
called himself the "last Romantic".
Like Matisse, he was a pupil of Gustave
Moreau and exhibited his paintings,
together with Matisse and other Fauves,
in the Salon d'Automne of 1905.
His resemblance to the Fauves, however,
is just an outward one – it does not
cover the subject matter of his paintings.
The colour scheme of his works is based
on deep blue, green and red shades and
is devoid of that decorative chromatic
brilliance which is characteristic of
Fauvist painting. Rouault's characters
are a whimsical mixture of saints and
outcasts — prostitutes, vagabonds,
mountebanks and clowns. Christ is for
him a symbol of the suffering of man
who has to live in an imperfect, sinful
world, a symbol of purity and solitude.

281
The General Staff building
By CARLO ROSSI (1775–1849)
The Toilet-Room of Count Nesselrode
Detail of the ceiling painting

The left wing of the General Staff building which has recently became the property of the Hermitage, in the 1820s housed the Ministry of Foreign Affairs and Finance. In the same place were the apartments of the first owner of these rooms, Chancellor Karl Nesselrode, who was responsible for Russia's foreign affairs for about forty years.
The Toilet-Room, similarly to some other living interiors, was adorned with an elegant painted decoration in the Empire style.

282
The General Staff building.
BY CARLO ROSSI (1775–1849)
The Ballroom. The living apartments of Count Karl Nesselrode. Detail

283
Mantel clock:
Education and *Vigil*
18th century. France
Bronze

This clock has a traditional
design: the dial is crowned
with the figure of an eagle
trampling lightning flashes –
attributes of the god Jupiter –
under its paws; the cornuco-
pias on either side of the dial
symbolize prosperity. Placed
below are the allegorical
female figures of *Education*
and *Vigil*. Between them is
a relief representation of royal
lions, vases and military
trophies.

284
The General Staff building
BY CARLO ROSSI (1775–1849)
**The Dining-Room. The living
apartments of Count Karl Nesselrode**

The display mounted in this room shows
costumes as part of the exhibition
"Beneath the Sign of the Eagle".
The showcases contain costumes
of a holder of the Order of the Holy Spirit
established by the French King Louis III
in 1578. The costume consisted
of a black velvet mantle with orange
lining, an embroidered cape of green
silk and clothes of black brocade.
The colours of the garments were
symbolic – green meant honour, love
and gallantry, while orange was
a symbol of the sun and gold.

285
The General Staff building
By Carlo Rossi (1775–1849)
The Ballroom. The living apartments
of Count Karl Nesselrode

The so-called Large Ballroom was one of the most impressive interiors
in the living apartments of Chancellor Nesselrode who, as the Minister
of Foreign Affairs, often gave large-scale state balls.
The room houses one of the most interesting sections of the exhibition "Beneath
the Sign of the Eagle"— articles in ormolu mounts produced at the workshop
of the celebrated French master, one of the world's leading bronze smiths Pierre
Philippe Thomire (1751–1843). Thomire's contemporaries admired his work
and rhymed his name with the verb *on admire*. The improvized tables are used
to display thirteen fine table decorations by the famous master.
On display in special show-cases is a collection of silverware by Jean-Baptiste
Claude Odiot (1763–1850) and Henri Auguste (1759–1816).

286 ▶
MAURICE DENIS (1870–1943)
The Story of Psyche
Panel 5 of the series *Cupid and Psyche*. 1908
Oil on canvas. 399 x 272 cm. Commissioned
by Ivan Morozov for the decoration
of his mansion in Moscow.
Entered the Hermitage in 1948 from the Museum
of New Western Art in Moscow

A series of decorative panels consisting of eleven paintings
and two ornamental borders was commissioned
by Ivan Morozov from Maurice Denis in 1907.
The fifth panel features the final scene of the Psyche legend –
Jupiter in the presence of gods bestows immortality upon
Psyche and celebrates her marriage with Cupid.
All the panels of the series are now put on display in the rooms
of the former General Staff building.

287
MAURICE DENIS (1870–1943)
The Story of Psyche
Panel 1 of the series *Cupid and Psyche*. 1908
Oil on canvas. 394 x 269.5 cm. Commissioned
by Ivan Morozov for the decoration
of his mansion in Moscow.
Entered the Hermitage in 1948
from the Museum of New Western Art
in Moscow

The theme of the first panel is the story of love
of Cupid and Psyche — Cupid flying by was
struck by Psyche's beauty. The series created
by Denis, which was surrounded in the rooms
of Morozov's mansion by elegant furniture,
ceramic vases and Aristide Maillol's sculptures,
set the tone in this superb Art Nouveau
ensemble.

Panoramic view
of the General Staff building
and Palace Square

INDEX

of Architects, Artists and Collectors

(figures in bold type indicate illustrations in the introductory articles;
Roman type refers to the plate numbers)

ЭРМИТАЖ

История зданий и коллекций

Альбом (на английском языке)

Издательство «Альфа-Колор», Санкт-Петербург, 2000
Тел./факс (812) 326-8384 E-mail: alfac@mail.wplus.net
(Серия ЛП № 000130 от 14 октября 1999)

Printed and bound in Finland